The Curious Case of the Three-Legged Wolf

EGYPT
Military, Islamism, and Liberal Democracy

By:
Dalia Ziada

Copyright © 2019
All Rights Reserved to The Liberal Democracy Institute, as the primary publisher and Dalia Ziada, the author.

Recommended Citation:
Dalia Ziada, "The Curious Case of the Three-Legged Wolf: Egypt's Military, Islamism, and Liberal Democracy" (The Liberal Democracy Institute of Egypt, 2019).

LDI

The Liberal Democracy Institute of Egypt (LDI), is a think tank dedicated to promoting democracy and fighting Islamic Extremism in Egypt and the Middle East.

www.egyldi.org

Contact the author:
dalia@egyldi.org

Contact the publisher:
office@egyldi.org

Contents

Introduction: **1**
Argument, Methodology, and Terminology

Chapter 1:   **15**
The Curious Case of Post-Arab-Spring Egypt
- ✓ What Makes Egypt's Case Unique?
- ✓ Egypt is not Tunisia

Chapter 2:   **30**
A History of Nonviolent Activism versus Violent Aggression

- ✓ Challenging Pharaoh King
- ✓ Submission to Islamic Conquest
- ✓ Al-Azhar, Nonviolent Resistance, and Liberalization
- ✓ Al-Azhar and the Military United
- ✓ Revolution 1919: Liberalization at All Fronts
- ✓ The Emergence of Political Islamism
- ✓ Revolution 1952: People and the Military United
- ✓ Nasser's Quest to Promote Communism
- ✓ The Revival of Political Islamism under Sadat

Chapter 3:   **60**
Mubarak's Three Decades of Illiberal Democracy
- ✓ *Mubarak's Strategy of Avoidance and Distraction*
- ✓ *Mubarak's Illiberal Democracy*
- ✓ *The Thriving of Political Islamism under Mubarak*
- ✓ *The Sacred Battle of Al-Azhar's Ahmed Al-Tayeb*
- ✓ *The Birth of the Liberal Democratic Movement*

Chapter 4:   **83**
Revolution 2011: Nonviolent Strategies between Skilled Dissent and Adept Military
- ✓ *Dragging Mubarak's Pillars of Support*
- ✓ *The Spark of the Nonviolent Revolution*
- ✓ *The Unique Dynamics of Revolution 2011*
- ✓ *Disintegrating Repressive Police Forces*
- ✓ *Confusions about the Nonviolent Military*
- ✓ *Mubarak's Fall into Prisoner's Dilemma*
- ✓ *The Foreign Affairs Role in 2011 Revolution*

Chapter 5:   **116**
From Mubarak's Super Long Autocracy to Muslim Brotherhood's Super Short Theocracy
- ✓ *How did the Muslim Brotherhood hijack the 2011 Revolution?*
- ✓ *Islamists' Extremely Disappointing One Year in Power*
- ✓ *The Spark of a Second Revolution*
- ✓ *Muslim Brotherhood's Violent Response Backfired*
- ✓ *The Big Lie of the Peaceful Rabaa Camp*
- ✓ *Declaring the Muslim Brotherhood a Terrorist Organization*

Conclusion: **168**
Lessons and Recommendations

Endnotes and References   **186**

The Curious Case of the Three-Legged Wolf

Introduction
Argument, Methodology, and Terminology

As ancient as history records, Egypt has always been a national state within naturally defined borders and unique demographic and cultural characteristics. The historical vigor of the Egyptian state, over six thousand years, depended entirely on balancing socio-political interactions between three dominating powers: the armed forces, the religious authority, and the grassroots' mobilizers. While the military's power is derived from weaponry and religious clerks' authority is commissioned by a divine power, the grassroots mobilizers learnt, over time, to empower themselves by using nonviolent tactics and strategies to gain legitimacy among grassroots citizens and influence decision-making at government level. Present-day Egypt, post the Arab Spring era, is similar to an old, yet strong, wolf standing on the same three legs: military, Islamism, and liberal democracy. The healthy interactions between the three socio-political powers during and after the Arab Spring played a great role in Egypt's survival of the dire consequences suffered by most Arab Spring countries. This research is answering the difficult scholarly question of why Egypt survived the Arab Spring, in comparison to Syria or Libya, through studying the violent and nonviolent strategic decisions made by the military, Islamists, and liberal democratic activists during and after the 2011 revolution.

The Argument:

The Arab Spring initiated a number of perplexing questions that occupied the minds and papers of academic researchers, for years. Most academia resorted to social theories and demographic analysis to decode the motives behind the casting waves of popular uprisings that overthrew hardliner dictators in major Arab countries, between 2010 and 2012. Yet, a few number of researchers dared to open the Pandora Box of the most confusing questions related to the aftermath of the Arab

The Curious Case of the Three-Legged Wolf

Spring revolutions. Academia found great difficulty in finding the actual factors, which prompted the outcome of each revolution in each of the Arab Spring countries to unfold into a completely different direction. While Libya and Yemen got drowned in bloody civil wars and Syria got occupied by the Islamic State terrorists, Egypt and Tunisia survived into preserving the unity of the national state and restoring public order under a valid system of governance. This research answers this difficult question through delving deeper into the curious case of Egypt's survival of the consequences of the Arab Spring.

In Egypt's 2011 revolution, the determining factor of revolution's success in toppling Mubarak, without affecting the coherence of the state, was not the high commitment to nonviolent discipline by the protesters, but the military's strategic choice to use "reverse nonviolent action," as an alternative to traditional violent repression, in containing the revolution and controlling its repercussions on security and politics. A closer study of the short-term tactics and long-term strategies used by the

Egyptian military, first, to contain liberal democratic activists during the 2011 revolution and, second, to weaken and disintegrate political Islamist groups during the conflict over political power after the revolution, enhances this argument. The Egyptian revolution suggests that the military, as one of the main pillars of support to the ruling regime, could determine not only the success or failure of a social uprising against a dictator regime, but also the flow and direction of political progressions following the fall of the dictator by a nonviolent revolution.

The relationship that was developed between the Egyptian military and liberal democratic revolutionists throughout the eighteen days of protests in Tahrir Square, in 2011, was a critical factor in the quick and tranquil fall of the authoritarian regime. Mubarak's regime depended heavily on two "weapon-carrying" pillars of support: the police forces, which existence depended on the existence of the regime, and the military institution, which enjoys financial and institutional independence. As the use of violence by police forces at the first three days of the revolution backfired into more heated protests, the military strategically chose to avoid violence and rather use "reverse nonviolent action" to show the will to appreciate and contain insurgency. The Egyptian case was unique in that it was not a traditional conflict of a nonviolent movement against an armed force. For the most part, the Egyptian revolution was a concerted nonviolent conflict between the nonviolent protesters and military forces that chose to put down their traditional weapons.

Academic scholars studying the Arab Spring developed four main propositions about why the military joined the challengers to Mubarak's regime in Egypt, as follows:

1. The military abandoned Mubarak because the military leaders had a personal interest in undermining Mubarak's plans to groom his son Gamal for the presidency because some rejected hereditary system and thought Gamal's economic power, as a

civilian, would threaten the officers' interests, so they chose to take advantage of the revolution to achieve that goal;

2. The military is an independent institution, and it is not necessarily dependent on Mubarak's patronage. The military chose to abandon Mubarak to preserve their legitimacy and their power on one hand and keeping the well-being of the state on the other hand;

3. The decision to disobey Mubarak's orders to kill the protesters was motivated by international pressure, especially from the friends of the Egyptian military leaders in the US military; and

4. The positive historical relationship between the military officers and the people made it harder for the military to kill the people and easier to disobey Mubarak.

The Curious Case of the Three-Legged Wolf

This research shall investigate into each of these propositions, through studying the political developments and contextual complexities that led to the 2011 revolution in Egypt and the power relations between military, Islamism, and liberal democrats in Egypt's modern history. The relationship between military forces' involvement and the success of a nonviolent revolution has been an interesting topic for academic research, for years. However, this research studies military's involvement through introducing *"reverse nonviolent action"* as a whole new theory in decoding military forces' behavior in response to a nonviolent revolution. The novelty of the topic, the special demographic, geographic, and historical characteristics of the Arab region, and the complicated history of violent conflicts and their influence on the progress of liberal democracy in the region, make the need for studying the relationship between military forces nonviolent response to nonviolent movements in this part of the world both urgent and challenging.

Methodology:

The research draws on two primary sources of information: (a) the growing literature on nonviolent strategies and tactics, with special focus on mechanisms used to undermine military power as one of the most crucial pillars of support for most dictators; and (b) interviews with key actors, including military officers and revolution leaders to investigate how the Egyptian military adopted a different approach in handling Mubarak, the liberal democratic revolutionists, and political Islamists. The investigations into the arguments offered by this research were conducted over a period of more than five years, extending from 2011 to mid-2017. During this period, Egypt and the Middle East witnessed massive changes in political interactions on domestic, regional, and international levels, which the research tried to include and integrate whenever necessary.

The Curious Case of the Three-Legged Wolf

Terminology:

<u>Introducing Reverse Nonviolent Action:</u>

This research introduces *"Reverse Nonviolent Action"* as a whole new theory in the academic field of nonviolent action and strategies. Reverse Nonviolent Action refers to the situation when the politically and militarily powerful opponents of the nonviolent movement make the strategic choice of deliberately using nonviolent tactics to maneuver the nonviolent tactics initiated by the nonviolent activists and reverse their results to the best interest of the opponent rather than serving the goals of the nonviolent movement. The Arab Spring Egypt is, purportedly, the first case in history where "reverse nonviolent action" is being applied. But before delving deeper into the curious case of Egypt, we need to agree on a clear definition to this new term, in comparison to other familiar terms in the field of studying nonviolent action and strategies: i.e.; nonviolent action, nonviolent sanctions, and counter nonviolent sanctions.

Dalia Ziada

The term ***"nonviolent action"*** is widely used to describe "a technique of struggle to control the power of rulers who are unwilling to accept voluntarily limits to their power."[1] The success of applying this technique depends on the nature of political power; that is "it has sources which may be restricted by withdrawal of cooperation and obedience" by the ruled subjects.[2] Political power is not limited to the rulers, who hold the political influence and military forces, needed to derive obedience from the subjects. On the contrary, political power is a "subtype of social power" that could be exercised by individuals or groups from outside the ruling regime to "change policies, to engage in opposition, to maintain the established system, or alter, destroy, or replace the prior power relationships."[3] In that sense, nonviolent action is a struggle, a means to proactively and effectively manage a conflict. Nonviolent action is not synonymous with pacifism, passivity, submissiveness.[4] It is a "force more powerful" that has "worked against all types of oppressive opponents."[5] Nonviolent action is a technique of struggle that includes a number of tactics and methods, which include: nonviolent resistance, nonviolent intervention, and nonviolent sanctions.

The term **_"nonviolent sanctions"_** is widely used by scholars, in the field of nonviolent action and strategies, to mean a set of "disruptive actions and aggressive measures to constrain or punish opponents and to win concessions."[6] Gene Sharp, however, describes sanctions as "ruler's punishments for disobedience."[7] In other words, the application of sanctions is not limited to those who hold the political power in the face of the disobedient nonviolent activists. This could be particularly true if seen in light of Sharp's description of political power as a "sub-type of social power."[8] Hence, sanctions can be applied in one of two forms: violent (e.g. practicing physical repression) or nonviolent (e.g. withdrawal of obedience and cooperation). However, it is important to note that "the nature of the sanctions applied in conflicts and for enforcement has a close casual connection to the degree of concentration or diffusion of power in the society."[9]

Dalia Ziada

The term **_"counter nonviolent sanctions"_** has been rarely used in academic literature on nonviolent action and strategies. Gene Sharp used the term only once in his masterpiece "Social Power and Political Freedom" published in 1980, as part of a bigger argument of the abuse of nonviolent sanctions by immoral actors for unjust purposes; as follows:

> *"Nonviolent sanctions have been used for purposes which many people would call unjust, and on occasion nonviolent challenges to established elite have been met with counter nonviolent sanctions or with other responses that did not involve violent repression. These developments have disturbed some people, especially persons who hold that only people who believe in an ethical or religious system enjoining moral nonviolence should or can use nonviolent action. Demonstrably, others can and have used nonviolent sanctions often with initial effectiveness."*[10]

Then, Sharp argued that the use of nonviolent sanctions and counter nonviolent sanctions, even for "unjust" causes or by the players on the "wrong" side of the political conflict, is better than using violent sanctions. "Nonviolent sanctions, compared to violent ones, tend to... affect, profoundly, the course of the conflict by reducing escalating physical and social destruction, and introduce very different dynamics with less harmful and even beneficial results."[11]

Nevertheless, the term **_"reverse nonviolent action"_** proposed in this research as a new theory in the scholarly debate around nonviolent action and strategies, holds a different meaning from the three widely-used terms as explained above. Reverse nonviolent action is a strategic technique used by military power to contain a nonviolent movement or win a conflict over political power. If the goal of nonviolent action is to redefine power relations in society, then the goal of reverse nonviolent action is to reverse the end-results of a nonviolent conflict against the socially empowered nonviolent disobedience.

It is an advanced stage of the strategic game of nonviolent action that starts after the nonviolent disobedience achieves a tangible progress or proven success in disempowering a political regime. Hence, Reverse nonviolent action is not a mere response or an immediate reaction by the power-holders to a nonviolent tactic employed by disobedience against them. Neither, Reverse nonviolent action is not a "nonviolent sanction" or a "counter nonviolent sanction" that is aimed at containing or disbursing the coherence of the nonviolent disobedience, or to give power back to the disempowered political regime. Rather, reverse nonviolent action is "the political alternative to war,"[12] which Gene Sharp tried to portray in his research, four decades ago. It is a long-term strategy of deliberately using proactive nonviolent tactics with the purpose to win a long-term conflict over political power against a popular nonviolent movement.

Chapter 1

The Curious Case of Post-Arab-Spring Egypt

The Arab Spring started before 2011, as a potential Middle East Spring. The Tunisian and Egyptian revolutions were not the first uprisings against dictatorship in the Middle East. In June 2009, young pro-democracy activists in Iran ran and maintained massive protests all over the country, which had effectively shaken the throne of Ayatollah.[13] The nonviolent uprising in Iran was launched and organized by Internet savvy young activists, under thirty years old, who represented more than 60% of the Iranian population. Activists in Egypt were following the developments in Iran with much hope that "if the revolution succeeds in Iran, the next revolution will take place in Egypt."[14] There were many similarities between the struggle for democracy and youth movements in both countries. However, the brutal interference of the military, especially the state-sponsored Islamic militia known as "Basij Forces," helped the Mullahs contain the uprising and remain in power.

Sixteen months later, the Tunisians started a nonviolent revolution that ended Ben Ali's rule in less than one month, followed by an Egyptian revolution that brought down Mubarak's thirty years of dictatorship within only eighteen days. The military's cooperation with nonviolent movements in Tunisia and Egypt during the 2011 revolutions played an essential role in guaranteeing the success of both nonviolent revolutions. "Cooperation" does not necessarily mean that the military believed in the goals and legitimacy of the revolution, but even the "negative cooperation" that included choosing not to kill protesters was enough to bring down the dictators, in both Tunisia and Egypt, by allowing the movements to continue to mobilize supporters and undermine the legitimacy of the authoritarian regimes.

Following Egypt, massive nonviolent uprisings erupted in Yemen, Libya, and Syria, each with varied responses by the military and insurgents. In the Arab Spring's successful cases – e.g. Egypt and Tunisia – both the protesters and the military strategically chose to use nonviolent action for offense and defense. In Libya and Yemen, revolutionaries used violence to defend themselves against the brutality of Saleh's and Gaddafi's military forces.

What Makes Egypt's Case Unique?

It is worth noting that the political situation in Egypt, prior to 2011 revolution, was ripe for change. A range of conditions helped the nonviolent movement succeed in record time. In Iran's 2009 revolution, the protesters were highly organized and skillfully applied nonviolent tactics and strategies against the regime. But their revolution failed because the proper conditions were not present, and the movement's momentum was not strong enough to prevail. The conditions were much more favorable in the Egyptian case; that included: international interest and pressure on military leaders not to practice violent repression on protesters, the independence of the military institution from the political regime, and the non-negotiable legitimacy of the nonviolent movement against the highly oppressive police forces and the corrupt regime. At the same time, there was a very narrow gap of conflicting interests between the military and the people, especially towards the end of the eighteen days of the revolution. Several of these conditions contributed to the restraint exercised by the Egyptian military toward nonviolent protestors and ultimately the military's active involvement in deposing Mubarak.

Egypt's survival from the consequences of the Arab Spring, through the smart and careful employment of nonviolent action and strategies, as well as reverse nonviolent action, is a particularly curious case. Like other Arab Spring countries, Egypt witnessed a ruthless conflict between its dominating social-political powers during and after the drumming waves of the Arab Spring. The sudden vacuum in political power after living under dictatorship regimes for long decades makes civil wars inevitable and

The Curious Case of the Three-Legged Wolf

unavoidable. Yet, Egypt's post-dictator civil war was a completely non-traditional one. The conflicting powers (e.g. liberal democratic revolutionists, Islamists, and the military) made an implicit choice to exhibit higher nonviolent discipline in managing their conflicts. Most Arab Spring scholarship ignores the role of reverse nonviolent action in Egypt's survival and development during and after 2011 revolution. They, rather, explain Egypt's survival from the consequences of the Arab Spring, through comparing it to Tunisia; demographically, politically, and sometimes historically. However, comparing Egypt to Tunisia, in that particular case, poses a huge scholarly fault.

Egypt is not Tunisia:

Ironically, Mubarak was quite precise when he said "Egypt is not Tunisia;" on his first address to the angry citizens rebelling against him, in January 2011, inspired by the Tunisians who succeeded in overthrowing Ben Ali, a week before. There are huge differences in the social, political, and demographic characteristics of both countries, the real motivation behind the revolution in each of them, and the potential of the eruption of violence, which each of the two countries had to handle at the time of the revolution and beyond. In fact, what makes the role of nonviolent action, and reverse nonviolent action, in Egypt's curious case of survival from the aftermath of the Arab Spring, worthy of thorough study and investigation is the simple fact that Egypt's demographic and political characteristics make it, according to that common criteria of stability adopted by most scholars, much closer to the violent scenario of Libya and Syria, more than it is to the serene flow of power transition, which took place in Tunisia.

Risk Factor 1: The Demographic Inhomogeneity:

Let's start by looking at the demographic characteristics of Egypt and Tunisia, and analyze the risk factors of violence, which these characteristics imply, in the absence of political order. There is a consensus amongst Arab Spring scholars that tribalism and inhomogeneous

The Curious Case of the Three-Legged Wolf

demographic mixture of the citizens of certain Arab Spring countries (e.g. Syria, Libya, and Yemen) played a role in sparking civil wars in those countries after the fall of their authoritarian regimes, which were keeping order by firming a tyrannical grip. Thus, they claim that Arab Spring countries, Egypt and Tunisia, survived the civil war scenario only because they are more demographically homogeneous or historically nation-oriented than other collapsing Arab Spring countries. However, such faulty claims can be easily busted by highlighting the fact that Egypt is not a homogenous society; at least not as homogenous as Tunisia.

The first risk factor of violence to be considered, here, is the massive difference in the size of population and percentage of active youth citizens and their level of education, in each of the two countries. Tunisia entered the Arab Spring with a population of ten million people, compared to over ninety million citizens in Egypt – the most populous country in the Middle East. In 2010-2011, the percentage of youth under thirty years-old in Tunisia was close to twenty-nine (29) per cent;[15] that is about three million people. In Egypt, in 2010-2011, the youth population sky-rocketed as high as thirty-nine (39) per cent; that is about forty million people. In other words, the youth population in Egypt alone is as four times as big as the whole population of Tunisia. Finding moral and political agreement and keeping nonviolent discipline, among three million people, from the same country and age group, is definitely much easier than finding agreement or establishing high nonviolent discipline among forty million young Egyptians, during the extremely chaotic and uncertain situation of the Arab Spring.

Risk Factor 2: The Complex Religious Anatomy:

The second important risk factor of violence to consider, in the comparison between the Arab Spring cases of Egypt and Tunisia, is the religious homogeneity and the level of religious piety; i.e. how big is the influence of religion and religious leaders on average citizen's views and decisions.

In Tunisia, Muslims are ninety-eight (98) per cent of the population, and the overwhelming majority of the Muslims are Sunni. All the Sunni's in Tunisia follow the doctrines of Imam Malik. The remaining two (2) per cent are Christians (mostly Roman Catholic), Jews, and Baha'is.[16] In comparison, Egypt has a more complex religious anatomy.

In Egypt, eighty-six (86) per cent of the population are Muslims.[17] The overwhelming majority of Egyptian Muslims are Sunni and less than one per cent of population is Shia. The Sunni majority are divided into four groups: Hanafi, Maliki, Shafi', Hanbali. Al-Azhar Mosque, the highest Muslim authority in Egypt and the Muslim world, follows Al-Asha'ari and Maturidi theological schools, but also teaches the doctrines of the aforementioned four schools.[18] Egyptian Christian citizens represent about twelve (12) per cent of the population. The majority of

Dalia Ziada

Egyptian Christians are Coptic Orthodox, but there are also hundreds of thousands of Egyptian Christians who follow other churches; including: the Armenian Apostolic, the Catholic (Armenian, Chaldean, Greek, Melkite, Roman, and Syrian Catholic), Maronite, and Orthodox (Greek and Syrian) churches. Add to this the Protestant community, which includes 16 Protestant denominations: Presbyterian, Anglican, Baptist, Brethren, Open Brethren, Revival of Holiness (Nahdat al-Qadaasa), Faith (Al-Eyman), Church of God, Christian Model Church (Al-Mithaal Al-Masihi), Apostolic, Grace (An-Ni'ma), Pentecostal, Apostolic Grace, Church of Christ, Gospel Missionary (Al-Kiraaza bil Ingil), and the Message Church of Holland (Ar-Risaala). There are also followers of the Seventh-day Adventist Church, about 1,500 Jehovah's Witnesses, and small numbers of Mormons. Egyptian Jews are approximately 125 senior citizens. Despite their very small number, they are divided into two groups, in Cairo and Alexandria, with two different leaders and plenty of disagreements. Finally, the Baha'i population estimates up to 2,000 citizens.[19]

[handwritten annotation: That's because they are remnants of much larger communities (~80,000 Jewish Egyptians) that were destroyed in a series of violent attacks, mass imprisonments, expulsions from the 1930s to the 1970s, most of the community members fled to Israel.]

The Curious Case of the Three-Legged Wolf

Risk Factor 3: Role of Religion in Shaping Politics:

Let's look at the religious piety factor. Tunisia is perceived as the most secular Arab country.[20] Religious piety and religious leaders have no real influence over the course of life of Tunisian citizens. Tunisia's Francophonie oriented culture mixed with decades of government preaching of secularism as an inclusive way of governance, in an attempt to push back the intrusion of political Islamist groups,[21] are main reasons for this high secular orientation in Tunisia, despite the fact that the ultimate majority of citizens are Sunni Muslims. As a result, there has always been a clear separation between religion and politics, in Tunisia. Religious leaders in Tunisia have no political influence and usually abstain from shaking hands, neither above nor under the table, with political power. Likewise, the low religious piety of the mostly secular Tunisian population, made it infeasible to the dictatorship regime of Ben Ali to think of using religious leaders as pillars of support.

In contrast, religion is piece and parcel of everyday life for Egyptians. An average citizen in some rural town in Upper Egypt or Delta region, who resembles the majority of population, would trust and obey the neighborhood church's Pastor or mosque's Imam more than they follow the orders or instructions of their local governor or Member of Parliament. Therefore, religious leaders, either on the official or the non-official side of the state, were heavily invested in politics to the extent that they found it easy to label themselves as in support or in opposition to the political regime. For decades, Mubarak relied on The Coptic Church[22] and Al-Azhar[23] leaderships in promoting his political agenda to the general public. Before that, Sadat depended heavily on the non-official religious/political group of the Muslim Brotherhood in defeating the heated opposition he received from the communist supporters of his predecessor Gamal Abdel Nasser, when he tried to apply liberalist reform policies, in both economics and politics. Ironically, the Muslim

The Curious Case of the Three-Legged Wolf

Brotherhood killed Sadat, later on, when he convened a peace treaty with Israel.

In addition to the main-stream Islam, which Al-Azhar represents, and the political Islam, which the Muslim Brotherhood epitomizes, there is the Salafist movement, which stands on the very far right of the spectrum. Salafism in Egypt started in 1980s as a purely religious movement, that had no political goals or aspirations of any kind. The Egyptian Salafists copied the same concepts, teaching, doctrines, and even dressing style of the Wahhabi movement in Saudi Arabia. In a relatively short period of time, the Salafists succeeded in occupying the majority of mosques, especially amongst the poor and illiterate citizens in rural towns, which the official Muslim institutions of Al-Azhar and the Ministry of Awqaf failed to cover. In early 2000s, when the Mubarak regime softened its grip on the Muslim Brotherhood and allowed them to run for parliament, the Muslim Brotherhood decided to collide with the Salafists to make use of their vast influence on the religious piteous grassroots citizens, in rural and poor cities.

This cooperation between the Salafists and Muslim Brotherhood on manipulating religion for acquiring political gains continued until the fall of the Muslim Brotherhood regime in July 2013.

The aforementioned statistics strongly defy the widely promoted academic theories, which suggest religious and political homogeneity as a guarantee to survival after bringing down a dictator. Looking closely at the case of Egypt shows that it was easier for Egypt to slip into the trap of initiating violent conflict upon religious dissimilarities. At least, that is what most Arab Spring scholars suggest as a reason for the civil war in Syria, Libya, and Yemen. Yet, this violent break down over religious differences did not take place in Egypt, simply because of the high commitment to nonviolent discipline by liberal democratic revolutionaries, which forced the military to use reverse nonviolent action to contain the revolution and control its outcomes, and thus forced the Islamists to

The Curious Case of the Three-Legged Wolf

abandon the use of violence, temporarily though, to gain popular support in their quest to political power, after the 2011 revolution. Ironically, once the Muslim Brotherhood lost control over their followers and retoured back to using violence to manage their conflict with the military, after the fall of their regime in 2013, they lost terribly; as we will discuss in finer details later.

Chapter 2

A History of Nonviolent Activism versus Violent Aggression

Challenging Pharaoh King:

In ancient Egypt, the ruling Pharaoh used to firm his grip over power, through labeling himself as the supreme authority over the three socio-political pillars of power: religion, military, and grassroots' mobilizers. A pharaoh was not merely a king in the political sense of the word. His political merits as a ruler were derived from introducing himself to the public as a "god" or a "representative of god" with para-human capabilities as a ruthless military warrior, who offers security and stability to the general public throughout the land of Egypt. In parallel, the Pharaoh used to upsurge his popularity and maintain his god-like status through wittingly containing domestic grassroots mobilizers and nonviolent activists.

The Curious Case of the Three-Legged Wolf

The first documented labor strike in history took place in ancient Egypt, under King Ramses III.[24] It was the first incident, in history, of a well-organized and successful nonviolent tactic that forced the Mayor and the Pharaoh King to increase payment, in form of grains, to the labor and guarantee them less oppressive working conditions. This captivating story of nonviolent activism in ancient Egypt took place around 1800 B.C. The nonviolent activist, whom the story was named after, is "The Eloquent Peasant: Khun-Anup." Khun-Anup was a fearless human rights activist, who used nonviolent tactics to stand up for himself and fellow farmers, who were cheated out of their possessions, by corrupt government employees.[25] The activist farmer filed a complaint about the injustice they were facing to the chief steward, who ignored him. Hence, he decided to launch a grassroots campaign using his poetic skills to petition his complaint to the king, through highlighting the rules of Ma'et, the goddess of rights and justice. At first, the king ignored his petition. But, the farmer continued his struggle and re-approached the king with eight different petitions, pleading his rights from different eight angels of justice and righteousness. Eventually, the king was intrigued by the persistence and eloquence of the activist farmer and took necessary measures to relieve the oppression practiced on peasants and end the practices of corruption by government officials.

Submission to Islamic Conquest:

Many thousands of years later, in 640 A.D., The Islamic Army led by Amr Ben El-As invaded Egypt and announced it as part of the Islamic Caliphate. The Islamic political system was not any different in the way it handled the three actors of power in Egypt. The Caliph, or the "Prince of Believers," was not only a political leader, but also "a soldier of Allah", who earns his credits to rule as a devout representative to Allah and the Prophet, by leading a ruthless army to invade and occupy new lands in Arabia and North Africa, under the flag of Islam. Surprisingly, there is no proof of any form of nonviolent activism during the dawn of the Islamic era in Egypt. This is perhaps due to the difference of the nature of political power in Islam, which consequently affected the dynamics of political and social relations. In other words, winning the satisfaction and approval of grassroots citizens was not a concern for the Islamic regime, as the Caliph usually expect blind obedience from the ruled subjects. As argued in the introduction above, the success of nonviolent action is provisioned by the nature of political power and whether "it has sources which may be restricted by withdrawal of cooperation and obedience."[26] Islamic governance system does not honor the concept of national state. The Islamic Caliphate treated all the states, which it occupied then, including Egypt, as a territory affiliated to the widely-spread Caliphate, not as individual states. This resulted into creating a form of political power dynamic that was impossible to challenge by ordinary grassroots citizens, not even with using nonviolent activism.

Al-Azhar, Nonviolent Resistance, and Liberalization:

In the 18th century, however, a new wave of grassroots nonviolent activism re-emerged in Egypt, by reputable Muslim scholars of Al-Azhar University, in response to frequent foreign invasions and Ottoman oppression. During that era, Egypt was part of the Ottoman Empire. The Egyptian people were impoverished and forced to work as farmers and servants to the super wealthy families of the Ottoman occupiers. A few Egyptians were able to send their male children to study at Al-Azhar University, to graduate as religious scholars and skip the ill fate of their poor fathers. At that era, Egyptians never had an armed force or a military system of their own. Egyptian males were not allowed to join the "Mamluk Army," which the Ottoman Empire composed from paid warriors randomly selected from different countries in South Europe and South West Asia. The franchise of the Mamluk army sent to Egypt, at that time, acted as both the police and military force, which gave them a hardliner scope of power, which they extremely abused in oppressing the helpless Egyptians. The

The Curious Case of the Three-Legged Wolf

Mamluk Army collected exaggerated taxes from grassroots citizens, using physical aggression and punishment to force payment and prevent the slightest potential of rebellion.

Umar Makram (1750-1822), a brilliant religious leader and graduate of Al-Azhar, was extremely offended by the oppression practiced by the Mamluk and decided to do something about it. In 1790s, he launched a successful nonviolent campaign to encourage grassroots citizens to stand up against the physical repression practiced by the Mamluks against them. His campaign weakened the Mamaluks' authority and affected their popularity in the eyes of the Ottoman Caliphate, as effective hardliner governors. This successful campaign heightened Makram's reputation as a political activist, not only as a religious leader. Grassroots Egyptians were fascinated by his courage and determination and unconditionally followed and trusted him.

In 1798, when the French Army, commanded by Napoleon Bonaparte (1769 - 1821), invaded Egypt,

Umar Makram organized the weaponless impoverished grassroots citizens into another nonviolent campaign to resist the French conquest. Surprisingly, Makram's nonviolent resistance campaign forced the mighty French army to withdraw from Egypt, in 1801.

As Umar Makram's political power and popularity grew, he was approached by Muhammed Ali, the Albanian Military Commander sent by Ottomans to restore peace in Egypt after the French withdrawal. Together, Ali and Makram made a plan to mobilize Egyptians to revolt against Khorshid Pasha, the Ottoman governor of Egypt. In 1805, the nonviolent campaign succeeded in toppling Khorshid Pasha and thus ending the Ottoman occupation of Egypt. Soon after, Muhammed Ali became the new Ruler of Egypt, who enjoyed massive grassroots citizens' approval and support. Ironically, the first decision Ali made, as soon as he seized power, was to exile Umar Makram out of Cairo and prevent him from practicing politics or grassroots activism. Apparently, he felt

The Curious Case of the Three-Legged Wolf

threatened by Makram's resilience and growing reputation as unbeatable religious leader and political activist.

Muhammed Ali took modernizing Egypt as his primary mission and challenge. He started by improving the economic system and life standard of ordinary Egyptians. Then, he created a secular education system, beside the already established religious education system in Al-Azhar, and sent the most brilliant students at both secular and religious schools to continue their graduate study in Europe. Meanwhile, he built theaters and opera houses and invited artists from Europe to perform in Egypt. Yet, his most important achievement was building a strong Egyptian military system composed of highly skilled and well-trained Egyptian males.

The students sent to Europe returned to Egypt with new liberal ideas and perceptions. Some of them turned into social activists and tried to influence liberal change in the Egyptian society. One prominent liberal activist, who appeared at that time and revolutionized the way society was thinking about women's rights and freedom of thought, was a religious leader graduating from Al-Azhar; called Refaa Al-Tahtawy (1801 – 1873). Al-Tahtawy's journey as a liberal activist started when he was sent with a delegation of forty Egyptian military officers to France, in 1826. He was the religious leader of the delegation, and he was only 25 years-old, at that time. He returned to Egypt, five years later, with a whole new approach about life that was more liberal and more supportive of individual freedoms and women's rights. He, then, became a liberal activist and launched a whole new educational and cultural movement, which he called "the Cultural Renaissance of Egypt."

Al-Azhar and the Military United:

One of Al-Tahtawy's most brilliant associates, Muhammed Abdo (1849 – 1905), who was also a prominent religious leader, graduate of Al-Azhar, and liberal human rights activist, started what we know today as the Egyptian civil society. He took on his shoulders the burden to continue the cultural renaissance initiated by Refaa Al-

The Curious Case of the Three-Legged Wolf

Tahtawy, promote human rights and defend women's rights, as well as encouraging Egyptian grassroots citizens to be more involved in social and political activities. Muhammed Abdo's growing popularity and influence encouraged Ahmed Urabi (1841-1911), a rebellious military commander in the newly formed Egyptian Army, to seek his help in mobilizing a nonviolent resistance campaign against Khedive Tawfik, the ruler of Egypt, who sold Egypt's wealth to the British and the French. That was the first actual cooperation between the military and Islamic leaders from Al-Azhar, in Egypt's modern history.

In 1878, Urabi supported by Abdo led a successful grassroots nonviolent campaign to protest a new law preventing the children of Egyptian peasants from joining the military forces. The campaign built up rapid and strong support all over Egypt, and turned into a grassroots revolution against the Anglo-French dominated regime of Khedive Tawfik. The law was repealed, and Urabi formed the first Egyptian political opposition party; with the name *"The Egyptian Nationalist Party"* which members included mostly military officers from the Egyptian army and politically active Islamic scholars from Al-Azhar. In 1882, the British army occupied Egypt and declared it as a protectorate of the British Empire, and then exiled Urabi to Ceylon.

Revolution 1919: Liberalization at All Fronts:

Urabi's exile caused a vacuum in the leadership of the nonviolent grassroots movement. As a result, a new wave of Egyptian nationalist activists emerged as the leaders of the next struggle for social freedom and political reform. The new activist leaders were not military officers nor Al-Azhar scholars, but a mixture of elite bureaucrats, reputable professionals, and liberal writers and intellectuals.

Saad Zaghloul (1859 – 1927), was one of the most known faces of the new wave of the Egyptian socio-political activism, during that era. Zaghloul was a reputable Egyptian lawyer with solid business connections in Europe and great popularity among Egyptian peasants in Northern

The Curious Case of the Three-Legged Wolf

Egypt. He became popular as a political activist thanks to his early efforts, using his international professional reputation and worldwide business connections, to mobilize the international community against the Great Britain to declare Egypt as an independent national state. In 1919, after Zaghloul founded Alwafd Liberal Party, the government of the British occupation, offended by his international advocacy against them and growing popularity among Egyptians, decided to exile him to Malta. Zaghloul's exile angered his local affiliates, who mobilized grassroots citizens into a nation-wide nonviolent revolution, which forced the powerful Great Britain to give up and eventually recognize Egypt's independence in 1922. One year later, in 1923, Zaghloul and his Alwafd Party dominated the new government and wrote the first-ever Egyptian constitution, as the basis for building a new liberal democratic state.

This new liberal era witnessed the birth of a more secular culture among the grassroots citizens. Jewish and Coptic Christian citizens began huge business investments, which gave a boost to the economy, and increased their influence on political decision-making. Meanwhile, a robust feminist movement led by Hoda Shaarawy (1879 – 1947) started to form, calling for women's equal rights to education, work, and political participation. In 1924, the movement organized a huge protest downtown Cairo, wherein the female leaders took off their head-scarves as a sign of social and intellectual liberation. Besides, Egypt started to gain a reputation as the "Hollywood of the East;" as it became the biggest cultural hub for filmmakers, artists, singers, poets, and creative writers from all over the Middle East.

During and immediately after World War I, many Europeans immigrated to Egypt, where they settled in peace, built homes, and ran profitable businesses. As the majority of Egyptians started to interact more positively with the newly adopted liberal and secular concepts in the social and political contexts, they lost interest in following religious leaders of Al-Azhar or military leaders from the Egyptian Army. People did not give up on their religious piety or admiration to the military, though. Most Egyptians maintained religious rituals and practice, in private, and most of the Muslim citizens labeled themselves as Sufi Muslims. Meanwhile, the World Wars I and II forced the military to focus more on war matters and much less on influencing domestic political affairs. In other words, the political activism role of religious and military leaders retreated to avail more space for liberal politicians and secular intellectuals to lead the general public.

The Emergence of Political Islamism:

Some religiously and socially conservative families, in rural cities, could not keep up with the swift modernization of life in the capital city of Cairo. Among them was the family of Ahmed Al-Banna, a Watchmaker in Behira, northern Egypt, who studied Islamic Sharia at an ultra-conservative Islamic school affiliated to Ibrahim Pasha Mosque in Alexandria. Al-Azhar had a very limited control and supervision over such non-official Islamic schools. Therefore, those schools found it easy to teach ultra-conservative concepts and interpretations of Islamic Sharia and holly texts.

The first student to Ahmed Al-Banna's conservative teachings about Islam was his own son, Hasan Al-Banna (1906 – 1949). As young as twelve years-old, the preparatory school student initiated the "Association to Fight Vice Deeds" with some of his school peers. In the name of the association, they organized public speeches at the village's mosque about Islamic Sharia law and sent letters to the religiously non-committed citizens, whom they labeled as "sinners" to urge them to stop drinking Alcohol or hanging in bars. Through this early and intense episode of local community activism, Hasan Al-Banna built the confidence and the skills to start a religious-political movement promoting Islamic Sharia as a system of political governance.

Immediately after graduating the "Teachers Training Institute" in Cairo, in 1927, Hasan Al-Banna was appointed as a teacher of Arabic language to primary school pupils in Ismailia, eastern Egypt. In that coastal rural

The Curious Case of the Three-Legged Wolf

town, where people were completely detached from the modern and secular lifestyle in the capital city of Cairo, Al-Banna found a fertile ground for expressing his rejection to "the Western model of secular democratic government, which contradicted his notion of universal Islamic rule."[27] In 1928, Hasan Al-Banna established *"The Muslim Brotherhood"* a secret underground Islamic association with the mission to restore the unity of Islamic Umma under one Caliphate, where Islamic Sharia is the only form of governance. In less than two years, the highly skilled social activist, Hasan Al-Banna, was able to attract a massive number of supporters to the Muslim Brotherhood group in Ismailia and neighbor towns. Driven by extreme ambition, he decided to introduce the group to broader audience, all over Egypt.

In 1930, Al-Banna was transferred to work in another primary school in Cairo, upon his request. His presence in Cairo upgraded the Muslim Brotherhood into a political Islamist organization, which practiced resounding opposition to the liberal government of Alwafd Party. While

Al-Banna continued to follow nonviolent tactics and strategies to promote the Muslim Brotherhood's cause, he formed a secret militia from the young male members of the organization to use them when necessary to protect the group against government oppression. As Al-Banna's reputation grew, the Muslim Brotherhood's influence spread beyond Egypt to mobilize supporters from North Africa and South-East Asia.[28] However, the secret militia of the Muslim Brotherhood took the group out of its righteous path.

As the political pressure by the government on the Muslim Brotherhood increased, Al-Banna lost control over the secret militia of his organization. In late 1930s and early 1940s, the militia of the Muslim Brotherhood started to practice violence to pressure and disturb the government; including committing serial assassinations against high-profile liberal politicians. In December 1948, the Muslim Brotherhood militia assassinated Mahmoud Al-Nokrashy, the Prime Minister and a co-founder of Alwafd Party. In revenge, the government assassinated Hasan Al-Banna, in February 1949.

Unexpectedly, the Muslim Brotherhood as a political organization did not die by the death of its founder. With the growing political and security turmoil on both the international and domestic scenes, during and after World War II, the Muslim Brotherhood grew larger in number and space. The group's secret militia took the lead of the group and subsequently initiated more politically-motivated violent atrocities and promoted more Islamic radical discourse. Meanwhile, the liberal government became much weaker and less effective in managing King Farouq I, who permitted severe British intrusion in governance.

Revolution 1952: People and the Military United

Public anger against the policies of the liberal government and King Farouq I offered a great opportunity to the "Egyptian Communist Party", founded in 1923, to offer its socialist principles as an alternative to the failing king and shaking liberal government. The party intensified its activities targeting underprivileged young labor and rebellious university students, through producing printed publications and holding public gatherings. This led to the mobilization of a socialist movement among Egyptian youth from all backgrounds that flourished in the years between 1946 to 1952 by organizing several successful protests against the British interference, the liberal government, and the king. The momentum created by this socialist movement, coupled with the continued failure of the government, attracted a number of rebellious young officers at the Egyptian military. Together they formed *"The Free Officers Movement"* which successfully mobilized a nation-wide revolution in July 1952, leading to the end of British dominance, dethroning King Farouq I, and announcing Egypt as a republic under the presidency of General Mohamed Naguib.

The Curious Case of the Three-Legged Wolf

Nasser's Quest to Promote Communism:

Gamal Abdel Nasser (1918 - 1970) was the mastermind behind the 1952 revolution and the charismatic speaker of the Free Officers movement, whom the Egyptian public adored. Nasser dearly embraced the communist ideology and thus was hated by the Muslim Brotherhood, who viewed communists as a bunch of disbelievers, who poses a threat to their Islamic government agenda.

Muslim Brotherhood militia attempted to assassinate Nasser while he was making a public speech in Alexandria, in 1954. In revenge, Nasser put Mohamed Naguib under house arrest, and declared himself as the new president of Egypt. Immediately after he seized power, Nasser waged a merciless arrest and punishment campaign against the Muslim Brotherhood. The surviving members of the Muslim Brotherhood went underground or flee to Europe, Asia, and the United States, where they established new branches for the group as civil society organizations or charity associations, while waiting for the right moment to return back to Egypt.

After taking care of the Muslim Brotherhood, Nasser attempted to defuse the power of Al-Azhar and its religious leaders over the public citizens. He knew that Al-Azhar would intervene with his plans to promote the communist ideology in Egypt, especially that this ideology encompasses atheism and materialism in its core. But, he also knew that he cannot simply shut down the doors of Al-Azhar University or prevent Islamic education in Egypt, due to the high religious piety of the Egyptian people. He would have been hated, if he assigned himself as an enemy to Islam or Muslim scholars. Therefore, Nasser adopted a three-steps strategy to neutralize the political and social influence of Al-Azhar in both domestic and international arenas, as explained below.

First, Nasser controlled the media through forcing government monopoly over press, book publishing, and film industry. State-owned publishing houses and film production companies allocated a huge budget for promoting communism as the new religion to Egyptians.[29] Meanwhile, the imams of Al-Azhar were poorly introduced as marginal non-influential characters in movies, and Al-Azhar was brutally attacked by communist writers in widely-distributed books and newspapers. That participated in shaking the respect and honor of Al-Azhar's Islamic scholars in the eyes of the public.

Second, Nasser attempted to control the public rhetoric of Al-Azhar. First, he publicly criticized Al-Azhar leadership for not taking necessary measures to renovate its religious education curriculum to match the new political and social transformations to communism.[30] Second, he tried to control the content of Friday prayers, which Al-Azhar Imams used for centuries to address the public on religious, social, and political issues. Nasser issued a presidential decree to unify the topic of all Friday ceremonial services in all mosques all over Egypt. As a result, the government used to send preaches, pre-prepared by the government, to imams to recite at mosques on Friday service. The topics prepared by the government were as meaningless and irrelevant to Islamic preaching as "the guidelines of street traffic."[31]

Third, Nasser tried to shake the image and credibility of Al-Azhar in the eyes of the international community. Since it was founded in 971, Al-Azhar has always represented the highest authority for all Muslims, worldwide. However, Nasser aimed at downgrading this universal image of Al-Azhar by re-introducing the institution to the international community as a local religious society under the full control of the government, and the imams of Al-Azhar as employees for the government. So, he founded a civil cultural organization with the name "The Islamic Conference" and gave it the priority in representing Egypt at international religious events and Islamic summits, as an alternative to Al-Azhar.[32]

Nasser's strategy succeeded in marginalizing Al-Azhar and mollifying the influence of its scholars and imams on the public citizens. The communist movement flourished, as planned, and the socialist doctrines dictated most of the political and economic policies. The military institution, thus, became the main leader of all aspects of life for Egyptians, including not only political, economic, or war affairs; but also, cultural, media, and religious affairs. The several wars Egypt had to fight against Britain, France, and Israel, under Nasser, made the dominance of the military institution over politics and economy viewed as acceptable by local citizens and international allies.

The sudden death of Gamal Abdel Nasser, at age 52, in September 1970 by a heart attack, left everyone in Egypt and the Arab region at utter shock. Sorrow and loss was suffered by millions of Arab citizens and political leaders for long months, after his death. Ironically, Nasser was a dictator, who led a strictly totalitarian political regime, allowed no opposition to breathe under his iron fist, and failed to establish a feasible economic system. However, people were charmed by the Arab nationalist ideals he promoted as the basis for his decisions. His historical role as a leading member of the Free Officers movement, which inspired political change all over the Middle East region, at that time, made people forgive and forget his oppressive system of governance, and selectively remember his legacy as the founder of the Arab Republic of Egypt.

The Revival of Political Islamism under Sadat:

In October 1970, Mohamed Anwar El-Sadat, another leading member of the Free Officers movement was appointed as the new President of Egypt. Despite being contemporaries, Nasser and Sadat adopted completely different political ideologies. While Nasser dearly embraced nationalism and communism, Sadat promoted liberalism and open market economy as the most viable form of governance. While Nasser governed through totalitarianism, Sadat planted the seeds for multi-party politics and encouraged political opposition to act. While Nasser labeled Israel and the United States of America as enemies to Egyptians and Arabs, Sadat reached out to the West, became a strong ally to the United States and convened a peace treaty with Israel.

The Curious Case of the Three-Legged Wolf

Nevertheless, Sadat's short years in presidency were not as easy as Nasser's. People did not admire him as much as they were infatuated by Nasser. His political and economic reforms received much opposition from Nasser supporters, who viewed Sadat's liberal reforms as an attempt to erase Nasser's communist legacy.

In January 1971, only three months after Sadat was seated as president, socialists – who called themselves Nasserists, later on – organized street protests against Sadat's reform agenda, under the title of "People's Intifada [Uprising]." However, the Nasserist protesters could not maintain nonviolent discipline and their violent protests backfired, as a result. The police forces had to intervene with extreme repression to control the violent riots. The protests lost their legitimacy in the eyes of the public who rejected violence. As expected, Sadat seized the opportunity to turn the table on Nasserists. As a first step, he removed Nasserists from all powerful government positions and limited their interference in state affairs and decision-making. On the other hand, he had to come up with a viable and swift strategy to control the disturbing noise aroused by Nasserists against his regime, so he could proceed quietly with his liberal reform agenda. To control Nasserists, Sadat had no option but empowering the Islamists, whom were heavily suppressed by Nasser in his quest to promote the communist ideology. Sadat's strategy to empower Islamists against Nasserists comprised a big risk that he had to pay for by his own life, ten years later.

Sadat's strategy to use Islamism to defuse the power of Nasserists included two parallel streams of action. On one hand, he freed the members of the Muslim Brotherhood, whom Nasser previously imprisoned in his early years as president. Then, he allowed the members of the Muslim Brotherhood, who fled the country under Nasser to return back and start launching businesses of their own and practicing politics and Islamic preaching on a limited scale. On the other hand, Sadat re-empowered Al-Azhar as the sanctuary of moderate Islam and gave it credit as the highest religious authority to Muslims worldwide. Al-

The Curious Case of the Three-Legged Wolf

Azhar scholars were, once again, allowed to represent Egypt in international Islamic events. Sadat, also, gave hours of live air-time on national TV for scholars from Al-Azhar to freely address the public on religious and social issues of concern. Under Sadat, Al-Azhar scholars became television stars and public figures highly admired and respected by public citizens, in Egypt and Arab countries.

In parallel, Salafism, a new unexpected brand of Islamism that Sadat never planned to empower, started to plant its roots in Egypt, during this era. In 1970s - 1980s, tens of thousands of young Egyptians traveled to work in Saudi Arabia, after the reverberation of the Saudi economy as a result of oil fields discovery. Those Egyptians did not return to Egypt only with tons of cash, but also with their own version of the Islamic extremist Wahabism ideology and culture.[33] This was the de facto beginning of the Salafist movement in Egypt, which grew later as a trend of grassroots Islamic radicalization promoting mental and physical jihad against secularism and all forms of modern life.[34]

Sadat's strategy to suppress Nasserists by empowering Islamists was successful. In a record time, the majority of the citizens ditched every communist belief they once embraced under Nasser and started to adapt to Sadat's new style of governance and living. Yet, his own life was ceased by the Islamists he empowered. On the 6th of October, 1981, Sadat was assassinated by a member of the Muslim Brotherhood.[35] The horrible scene of assassinating Sadat was caught on the cameras of the national television, which was live-transmitting Sadat's participation in the annual celebration of Military Day.[36]

After Sadat's assassination, the Islamists got more powerful. The Muslim Brotherhood became stronger on both political and religious fronts. The Salafists grew in numbers and financial power, as they were generously funded by donations from Wahabist enthusiasts in Saudi Arabia. The Salafists allied with the Muslim Brotherhood to control the religious rhetoric against the moderate official rhetoric of Al-Azhar. New Islamic Jihad militia were formed in poor and rural cities in Upper Egypt. The rising threat of

The Curious Case of the Three-Legged Wolf

Islamists, in addition to a stumbling economy, was the challenge inherited by Hosni Mubarak, the Vice President of Sadat, who automatically became the president of the state after his assassination.

Chapter 3

Mubarak's Three Decades of Illiberal Democracy

Mubarak's Strategy of Avoidance and Distraction:

When announced as a president, immediately after Sadat's assassination, Mubarak did not waste much time, like his predecessors, trying to win the approval of the public. The Egyptian people already admired him long before he was seated as President. Mubarak was highly appreciated for catalyzing the peace talks with Israel in his capacity as the Vice President of Sadat, as much as he was cherished for his critical role in winning the 1973 war against Israel, in his former position as The Commander of the Air Force and Deputy Minister of Defense. However, Mubarak's biggest challenges as a new president were to improve the economy and control the expansion of Islamic Jihadists and political Islamists, who flourished under Sadat.

Mubarak adopted a strategy of "avoidance and distraction" to handle these domestic challenges, in addition to arising regional and international rattles.

On the international level, Mubarak kept open and balanced relationships with all major foreign powers who had a direct influence on Egyptian politics, regardless of the nature of power polarity in the international system. He followed Sadat's approach of keeping strong and healthy ties with the United States, which was essential for keeping US Aid funds and armament flowing in. Yet, at the same time, he kept prolific relations with the Soviet Union, Britain, and powerful European allies like France and Germany. He, also, strengthened relations with African countries, especially those sharing the Nile River with Egypt, in an attempt to neutralize their resentment for building the High Dam, under Nasser.[37] Mubarak, also, restored healthy relationships with Sudan, ending long years of diplomatic conflict over border cities between the two countries.

On the regional level, Mubarak started by renovating relationships with Arab countries, after most of them diplomatically boycotted Egypt in response to Sadat's rapprochement to Israel and the US. This was highlighted by Egypt's return to hosting the headquarters of the Arab League in 1982, a few months after Mubarak took power. Mubarak's appeal to Arab countries involved abandoning Israel as a close ally. Because of Egypt's commitment to the Peace Treaty with Israel, Mubarak could not announce Israel an enemy again. But, he kept the relationship with Israel at a status of "cold peace" by neither completely neutralizing political, economic, and social relationships, nor completely cutting connections or border cooperation with Israel. By adopting this status of cold peace with Israel, Mubarak hit more than one bird with one stone. First, he restored torn ties with Arab countries. Second, he kept the US Aid flowing into Egyptian economy as a result of his continued commitment to Camp David Accord.[38] Third, he kept the Egyptian people distracted from domestic troubles by amplifying the

Palestinian-Israeli conflict. Fourth, he used the Palestinian issue as a tool to justify his continued cold relationship with Israel, while at the same time playing the role of the big brother of Arabs, whom the west would always seek his partnership on solving Middle East problems. Actually, he successfully acquired this status, not only by mediating on the Palestinian Israeli conflict, but also by intervening in solving regional conflicts like the Gulf War, in 1991, between Iraq and Kuwait.

On domestic level, Mubarak's governance style was not any different from his international and regional strategies. At home, he opened the door to all parties to operate, as long as they do not threaten his presidency. On the positive side, this strategy opened the door to the liberal democratic movement and the civil society to transpire and blossom in a record time. On the negative side, this strategy allowed corrupt businessmen to prosper and corrupt the whole economic system. Even worse, this strategy enabled the Muslim Brotherhood and

Salafists to conquer the souls and minds of mostly uneducated grassroots citizens.

Mubarak's Illiberal Democracy:

Egyptians and international observers had always been confused by the state's performance, under Mubarak, which exhibited simultaneous rehearsals of democratization and authoritarianism. For example, Mubarak's government was the first in the region to provide citizens with affordable computers and easy access to internet service. Unlike Turkey, for instance, the Egyptian state never intervened or attempted to block any website, including blogging platforms used by dissidents and political opposition to criticize Mubarak or his government. However, Mubarak's regime did not shy from continuously harassing and arresting young bloggers and activists for whatever they publish online. The practice of torture against citizens by police forces was widely tolerated and encouraged by the regime. Another example on Mubarak's confusing style of governance had to do with how he handled political parties and civil society. While the state ran parliamentary elections regularly and allowed opposition parties and individuals to run for seats, the elections were usually manipulated to allow his National Democratic Party (NDP) to dominate the super majority of the seats. While the government did not explicitly ban the work of non-governmental organizations (NGOs), working on political and civil rights, the human rights advocates and activists volunteering at those NGOs were continuously harassed by police and labeled by state-owned media as spies to some foreign countries that fund their activities.

Under Mubarak, Egypt could have been considered neither a democracy nor an autocracy, but a living example of the concept of "illiberal democracy," first introduced by Farid Zakaria in his masterpiece "The Future of Freedom: Illiberal Democracy at Home and Abroad." According to Zakaria, the Athenian definition of democracy as "the rule of people" through the process of selecting their government is "meaningless" if it is not supported by constitutional liberalism that would guarantee the fairness and openness of practicing democracy.[39] He wrote:

> "if a country holds competitive multiparty elections we call it democratic. When public participation in a country's politics is increased – for example through the enfranchisement of women – this country is seen as having become more democratic."[40]

One interesting instance highlighting Mubarak's use of this astute strategy of governing through illiberal democracy, took place in 2009, while the regime was preparing itself for the parliamentary elections of 2010. Mubarak's main goal was to lessen the number of seats seized by the Muslim Brotherhood in 2005 elections, and bring more of his supporters into parliament. Therefore, in 2009, Mubarak issued a presidential decree allocating sixty-four seats in the lower house of the parliament for women, and publicized the decision as a necessary intervention by the regime to encourage more women to

The Curious Case of the Three-Legged Wolf

participate in the 2010 parliamentary elections.[41] Thus, he hit two birds with one stone. On one hand, he polished the image of his regime in the eyes of the international community by showing that he is becoming supportive to women's right to political participation. On the other hand, his initiative effectively weakened the Muslim Brotherhood's parliamentary bloc, which occupied one-third of the seats in parliament in 2005, by replacing them with women parliamentarians loyal to the NDP and the regime.[42] Concurrently, the regime denied international observers access to parliamentary or presidential elections, claiming that allowing international observation on domestic elections would "infringe the national sovereignty."[43] In addition, grassroots movements and local nongovernmental organizations were deterred from observing elections by the Emergency Law, which remained in effect along the era of Mubarak, since the assassination of Sadat in 1981. The Emergency Law granted the president of the state "extraordinary powers to detain citizens prevent public gatherings, and issue decrees with little accountability to Parliament or the people."[44]

The Thriving of Political Islamism under Mubarak:

While Mubarak was ruthlessly successful in fighting Jihadist Islamists, he availed a huge social and political space to political Islamists from the Muslim Brotherhood and the Salafist movement. The Muslim Brotherhood used charity work, extensively and intensively, to attract the political support of grassroots citizens at poor and rural cities, where the government failed, terribly, to provide basic medical and social services.[45] In parallel, the Salafists dominated mosques, and accordingly leveraged their religious authority over illiterate citizens in the rural towns, where the Muslim Brotherhood were already highly active and effective. Together, the Muslim Brotherhood and the Salafists, through manipulating people's religious piety, lack of education, and basic human needs, managed to gather supporters to their political agenda of abandoning the secular government and ruling by Islamic

Sharia. Ironically, the state-owned media used to label the Muslim Brotherhood as the "banned group," while Mubarak's government had never taken a single viable decision to stop the group from being overtly active on religious, social, and political fronts. The police state security forces used to harass and arrest members and leaders of the Muslim Brotherhood, while the government had never really shut down Muslim Brotherhood's media stations or charity organizations.

This mouse and cat relationship between Mubarak's regime and the Muslim Brotherhood did not serve Mubarak as much as it benefited the Brotherhood, in particular, and political Islamism, in general. In 2003, before Mubarak had realized it, the Muslim Brotherhood found their way to policy-makers in the United States' Administration and Capitol Hill, where they falsely introduced themselves as an Islamic, yet moderate, political opposition to Mubarak's regime.[46] The consequences of this move by the Muslim Brotherhood were translated later into US intervention to force Mubarak to allow the members of the Muslim Brotherhood to run for Parliament seats in the 2005 parliamentary elections. To Mubarak's surprise, the two decades of Muslim Brotherhood's charity work and Islamic preaching among the grassroots citizens enabled the Muslim Brotherhood to win one third of the parliamentary seats.

The Sacred Battle of Al-Azhar's Ahmed Al-Tayeb:

The religious, social, and political role of Al-Azhar witnessed a sharp decline during the first two decades of Mubarak's reign. That was not only because of the massive expansion of the Muslim Brotherhood and the Salafists among grassroots citizens, but also due to Mubarak's exaggerated control over Al-Azhar's leadership and autonomy.[47] However, this submissive state of affairs between Mubarak's regime and Al-Azhar changed, completely, by the appointment of Dr. Ahmed Al-Tayeb, a professor of Philosophy, as the President of Al-Azhar University in 2003, and then as the Grand Imam of Al-Azhar, in 2010.

The Curious Case of the Three-Legged Wolf

Quietly and wittingly, Al-Tayeb restored the lost respect and appreciation of Al-Azhar, on domestic, regional, and international levels. Under his leadership, Al-Azhar as a religious and academic institution returned back to participating effectively and influencing the course of socio-political developments happening in Egypt, during the last decade of Mubarak's era, as well as during and after the 2011 revolution. On his highly active seven years as the President of Al-Azhar University (2003 – 2010), Al-Tayeb was determined to restore Al-Azhar's international reputation and credibility, while winning the pitiless battle against the Muslim Brotherhood and the Salafists. In their quest to destroy the secular national state and replace it with an Islamic Sharia government, the Muslim Brotherhood and the Salafists regarded Al-Azhar as an inimical rival.

Al-Azhar is, arguably, the most effective utensil of Egypt's soft power in international affairs, and one of the most durable pillars of support to the national state. The wellbeing of Al-Azhar automatically weakens the influence of political Islamism, while the weakening of Al-Azhar opens a space for political Islamists and Islamic extremists to prosper and expand. That explains why the Muslim Brotherhood invested a lot of their energy and resources trying to destroy the credibility of Al-Azhar. On their so-called religious preaches to grassroots citizens, Muslim Brotherhood and their Salafist allies used to publicly attack Al-Azhar's scholars and imams by calling them the "Sheikhs of Sultan;" meaning that they are Mubarak's loyalists, who abuse religion to serve the agenda of the secular government.[48] In parallel, students and teachers at Al-Azhar University, who were members or affiliates of the Muslim Brotherhood, used to organize regular protests and sit-ins inside the university's campus, to disturb Al-Azhar's administration, level political pressure on the university's leadership, and shake the respect of Al-Azhar scholars in the eyes of the public.

The relentless offenses by political Islamists against Al-Azhar reached its peak, in December 2006, when the Muslim Brotherhood affiliated students upgraded

The Curious Case of the Three-Legged Wolf

their nonviolent protests by wearing Islamic militia outfit and performing a violent military show, inside the university's campus.[49] The leaders of the Muslim Brotherhood, who most of them were newly elected as Members of Parliament, at that time, attempted to disown the incident by cunningly justifying the militia show as a random unplanned reaction by angry students to the unresponsive administration of the university. However, this one reckless show of violence caused the group to lose a big portion of its grassroots and international support, while it gave the Mubarak regime a golden opportunity to squash Muslim Brotherhood leadership through putting them to military trials.

In his capacity as the President of Al-Azhar University, Dr. Ahmed Al-Tayeb initiated investigations into the militia show incident and submitted its conclusions to State Security Department. As a result, the police forces arrested forty leading members of the Muslim Brotherhood, including Khairat Al-Shatter, the group's most powerful funder and mastermind.[50] Between 2007 and 2010, almost all the leading members of the Muslim Brotherhood were subjected to various episodes of confinement and military trials.[51] Meanwhile, Al-Tayeb spent the months, following the militia show incident, in detoxing the university from the affiliates of the Muslim Brotherhood. He fired the students who participated in the militia show, prevented further protests or sit-ins from taking place inside the university campus, and removed the professors and administrative employees, affiliated to the Muslim Brotherhood, from policy-making positions inside the university.

This necessary detoxification and re-organization of Al-Azhar University gave Al-Tayeb a chance to resume his battle against Islamic extremists outside the walls of the university. He started by reaching out to national television to improve the content of Islamic shows by bringing on scholars from Al-Azhar to preach to the general public against the then widely-spread extremist discourse of political Islamists. In parallel, Al-Tayeb launched "the Medical Convoys of Al-Azhar" project, which allowed physicians and imams from Al-Azhar

The Curious Case of the Three-Legged Wolf

University to travel to poor rural areas, on a regular basis, to provide free-of-charge medical and social services to grassroots citizens. The main purpose of that effort was to free the grassroots citizens from the manipulation of the Muslim Brotherhood and Salafists, who abused charity work and religious piety to win the poor people's political support.

Nevertheless, Al-Tayeb did not give up on his equally important goal to refurbish Al-Azhar's international reputation and credibility. He started by including a post-graduate academic program that teaches Islamic studies in English to interested Egyptian or non-Egyptian individuals, whether they received their graduate education at a religious school or a secular college. In 2007, Al-Tayeb founded and managed "The World Organization of Al-Azhar Graduates" with the purpose to revive connections with Al-Azhar graduates, from foreign nationalities, and encourage them to act as ambassadors to Al-Azhar in their home countries.[52] Meanwhile, the association partnered with other universities and Islamic institutions, worldwide, on educating English language to Egyptian graduate students of Al-Azhar. Those particular efforts had a tremendous effect on Al-Azhar's reputation worldwide, and simultaneously upgraded the skills of Al-Azhar scholars and imams and improved their influence on Muslim rhetoric, at home and abroad.

The impressive success of Al-Tayeb in his role as the President of Al-Azhar University made him the most qualified candidate to the most prestigious position of the Grand Imam of Al-Azhar.[53] In March 2010, after the death of his predecessor, Mohamed Sayed Tantawy, Al-Tayeb was appointed as the Grand Imam. The new position helped him score more points of victory in his sacred battle against political Islamists. He went vocal on criticizing Salafist extremist beliefs, in general, and their discriminative fatwas against women, in particular.[54] He brazenly rejected two of the most controversial principles promoted by political Islamists to suppress women in the name of Islam: i.e. forcing women to wear Niqab as the so-called "Islamic dress" and the horrible practice of Female Genital Cutting on minor girls.[55]

Obviously, the Muslim Brotherhood was extremely offended by seeing Al-Tayeb on the top of Al-Azhar Institution. They launched fierce media campaigns against him, going as far as describing Al-Tayeb as a "Mubarak loyalist" who "hijacked" Al-Azhar to the benefit of the regime.[56] They even claimed that he is not qualified to the position of the Grand Imam because of his background as a professor of Islamic Philosophy.[57]

After the 2011 revolution, the Muslim Brotherhood tried by all means to remove Al-Tayeb from his position as the Grand Imam. The Supreme Council of Armed Forces (SCAF), which took political leadership after the fall of Mubarak's regime, refused to accept Al-Tayeb's resignation and insisted on keeping him in his position till a new constitution is written and a new state president is elected.[58] When Mohamed Morsi, of the Muslim Brotherhood, became the President of the State in mid-2012, the Muslim Brotherhood put a massive pressure on Al-

Tayeb to resign.[59] But, Al-Tayeb fought hard to keep his position, out of fear of letting the Muslim Brotherhood take over Al-Azhar's leadership, and thus use it to promote their extremist agenda. During that time, the young Judge Mohamed Abdel Salam, who acted as Al-Azhar's legal advisor, then, succeeded in winning tough negotiations with the Constitution Writing Committee to instate "total immunity against removal by the president of the state" for the position of the Grand Imam of Al-Azhar.[60] This leveraged the power of Al-Tayeb to continue his sacred battle against political Islamism, in Egypt and beyond.

The Birth of the Liberal Democratic Movement:

The liberal democratic movement in Egypt is relatively new. It appeared, roughly, around one decade before the 2011 nonviolent revolution, which was initiated and led by young liberal democratic activists under the age of thirty years-old. Most of the young liberal democrats started their journey of political activism as volunteers to civil society organizations. They resorted to human rights

The Curious Case of the Three-Legged Wolf

NGOs as an alternative to the so-called opposition parties. The communist agenda and the irrelevant Nasserist principles embraced by the old and decayed political parties, in addition to their shaming weakness in face of Mubarak's regime, did not appeal to the young activists, who believed in the glorious ideals of individual freedom and liberal democratization. Civil society organizations, promoting political and civil rights, were the only incubators to such ideals, at that time.

Ironically, the nonviolent struggle to bring down Mubarak and establish a liberal democratic state that respects human rights and civil freedoms started to sharpen by the unwelcomed appearance of Gamal, the son of Mubarak, on the political scene in 2003. He was introduced to the public as a potential successor to his father, which catalyzed the organized struggle for change by young political dissidents. Several nonviolent movements were formed, the most prominent of which were "Kefaya" in 2004 and "6 April" in 2008. Meanwhile, civil society across the Middle East was getting stronger thanks to the international interest – after the War on Saddam Hussein in Iraq – in enhancing pro-democracy and human rights nongovernmental organizations through funding and capacity building initiatives.

In an attempt to distract the young people from joining anti-Mubarak campaigns or human rights NGOs, while continue to please international powers by feigning support for freedom of expression; the Egyptian government decided to provide citizens with affordable access to mobile phone, Internet, and television satellite services. The year 2004 marked a technological revolution in the communications sector in Egypt, led by then Minister of Communication, Ahmed Nazif, who was appointed a few years later as the Prime Minister and kept that position until Mubarak fired him during the 2011 revolution. Unexpectedly, cheap access to the Internet helped the young Egyptian dissidents, human rights NGOs, opposition political parties, and pro-democracy movements to better organize and form more influential networks. In 2005, a vibrant community of bloggers started to flourish as the main source for credible information about Mubarak regime's corruption and violations to human rights. The internet medium and free blogging platforms enabled the young liberal democratic activists to form a community of their own. Blogging was the safe haven, where young activists found a space to express their ideas and discuss political issues they cannot discuss openly in the real world.

Young members of the Muslim Brotherhood and a few number of Salafi youth joined the blogging fever, at the time, too. Their primary goal was to convert the young liberal activists into embracing the ideals of the Muslim Brotherhood. Interestingly, the Islamist bloggers became more liberal in the process, and started to rebel against the oppressive instructions and extremist teachings preached by the leaders of the Muslim Brotherhood group and the Salafist movement. One Islamist blogger, for example, launched an online campaign to denounce the marginalization of women inside the leadership hierarchy of the Muslim Brotherhood.[61] On the other hand, despite the majority of the Salafist bloggers were interested in discussing religious issues related to Sharia and the holy texts, their views were relatively more liberal than the views of the elders of the Salafist movement.

Remarkably, the young liberal democratic activists, who started their political struggle with shy clicks and funny nicknames on the internet medium in 2005, ended up toppling Mubarak in a historical nonviolent revolution in 2011.

Chapter 4

Revolution 2011: Nonviolent Strategies between Skilled Dissent and Adept Military

Dragging Mubarak's Pillars of Support:

Before 2004, Mubarak relied on four main pillars of support: judiciary, parliament, military, and police. They helped him to stay in power through a centralized authoritarian state that wore a democratic mask. Mubarak, also, nurtured additional, but less important, pillars of support like the ruling National Democratic Party (NDP), the business community, and state-owned media.

In 2010, Mubarak attempted to manipulate the parliamentary elections, but had to do so without the help of one of his four main pillars of support, the judiciary, which abandoned him during the 2005 presidential and parliamentary elections by exposing the forgery of results by the NDP. Soon after the 2005 elections, a strong nonviolent movement was launched to call for the independence of the judiciary and establishing the rule of law.[62] The Independent Judges Movement was strongly supported by human rights NGOs, Kefaya Movement, and the Bloggers Community. Together, they formed a massive nonviolent front that began to irritate Mubarak and threatened his credibility in the international community.

In response, Mubarak empowered the police forces, especially State Security Department. The State Security forces were authorized, through the continued renewal of the Emergency Law, to harass activists, torture dissidents, and arrest whoever acted as a threat to the regime. Over the following five years, the brutality of police forces increased. They tortured civilians in police stations, streets, and even in their houses. State Security forces arrested bloggers and activists and tortured them to collect information about their movements and organizations, or put them in jail for years without bringing charges against them. This sustained repression over the decades triggered a growing consciousness within civil society about the need to resist the Mubarak regime.

As Mubarak lost the judicial system as a critical pillar of support, he had to rely more heavily on the Emergency Law and the brutality of the police to enhance his position. Meanwhile, the interest in ending corruption and dictatorship was on the rise. In an effort to counter this persistent repression intelligently and strategically, young activists used the Internet medium not only to organize but also to learn about the science of nonviolent action and strategies. The international interest in empowering Egyptian civil society helped NGO members to travel to the United States and Europe to acquire new skills and sequentially transfer knowledge about nonviolent struggle to their fellow activists at home. Several activists were educated about the history and theory of nonviolent civil resistance against corrupt regimes in 2007 – 2009 through the Fletcher School for the Advanced Study of Nonviolent Conflict and the International Center on Nonviolent Conflict, in addition to participating in training workshops on the application of these theories organized by the Center for Applied Nonviolent Action and Strategies (CANVAS).

In 2008, after the decline of the Kefaya Movement following internal conflicts between its leaders, the 6 April Movement was formed and started to apply nonviolent tactics to challenge Mubarak's regime. The logo of the movement (the right-hand fist) was an adapted version from the logo of the Serbian nonviolent movement Otpor that brought down Milosevic and a few years later established CANVAS. The founders of the 6 April Movement were formerly young members of Kefaya Movement and the electoral campaign to support the young liberal candidate, Ayman Nour, who ran for presidency against Mubarak in 2005. Ayman Nour was very close to victory over Mubarak, but a few months after the elections, Mubarak put him in jail, though his campaign remained strong and continued growing into a political opposition movement.

The Curious Case of the Three-Legged Wolf

Meanwhile, the controversy over the viability of the use of nonviolent action to bring down Mubarak started to emerge among thinkers, academics, and civil society members. The young activists who received CANVAS[63] and ICNC trainings held several training workshops and conferences and translated books from Gene Sharp and Peter Ackerman around the topic of nonviolent action and strategies.[64] In 2008, the writer of this book translated into Arabic an American comic book that was originally published in 1960s about the Montgomery Bus Boycott, and held a number of workshops in several Arab capital cities about the concept of nonviolent action using the comic book. In 2011, the translation of this book was given credit for inspiring young people in the Arab world to adopt nonviolent tactics to undermine dictatorial regimes.[65]

The Spark of the Nonviolent Revolution:

In August 2010, the Egyptian public, especially young people, were shocked and outraged by the news story of Khaled Said; a young underground musician from

Alexandria, who was beaten to death by two policemen outside a cyber café that he was visiting, after he refused to let the policemen search his belongings. This was not the first incident of police physically assaulting innocent citizens. But it was the most shocking because the victim was not a "criminal, a terrorist, or a thug"[66] and was publicly beaten in the street. The murder of Khaled Said poured gas on the fire of anger of the young people, who had been suffering from political marginalization and economic corruption. The murder of a young man, who looked like them, was like facing a mirror that exposed their helplessness in the face of the growing brutality of the regime. A few days after the death of Khaled Said, a Facebook page was created to call for the punishment of the policemen who killed him, ending the state of emergency, and urging police forces to stop using violence against civilians. In cooperation with other youth movements, like the 6 April Movement and human rights NGOS, the Khaled Said page organized several small but scattered rallies in Cairo and Alexandria that were widely covered by local bloggers and independent media stations and news websites.

Around the same year, Gamal Mubarak seemed like he had already established himself as a politician, after being hired as the Chief of Policies Committee at the ruling National Democratic Party (NDP). That was the first step in preparing himself to run for presidency, in the presidential elections that was planned to convene in late 2011. To guarantee a victory, he illegally intervened into organizing and then manipulating the results of the parliamentary elections of 2010. He forged elections' results to give the majority of parliament seats to his loyal affiliates from the businessmen community, the NDP, and Mubarak loyalists at the so-called opposition parties, who had negotiated a secret deal with the Mubarak regime.[67] It was shocking and unrealistic to observers, in Egypt and abroad, to see the Mubarak's NDP winning eighty-three per cent of parliament seats, despite rising rates of dissatisfaction and rejection to Mubarak and his government. In response, liberal democratic activists, civil society organizations, and young bloggers called for annulling the results of elections, under allegations of fraud. High profile officials and media outlets in the United States and Europe echoed Egyptians' worries.[68] However, the regime responded by declining their criticism as an unwelcomed foreign interference in Egypt's domestic affairs.[69] Arguably, the forgery of 2010 parliamentary elections backfired on Mubarak's regime, as it undermined the legitimacy of the new parliament and thus weakened the parliament as one of his most critical pillars of support.

Mubarak came to the end of 2010 relying on only two of his most crucial pillars of support, the military and the police, after he had already lost the legitimacy of parliament and the backing of the judiciary. The National Democratic Party and state-owned media were secondary pillars of support for Mubarak's regime. They were less important and much weaker than the aforementioned primary pillars of support; i.e. judiciary, parliament, military, and the police force. They could only hold Mubarak's regime standing for a few weeks, after the

The Curious Case of the Three-Legged Wolf

scandalously forged parliamentary elections in 2010 and the eruption of a nation-wide nonviolent revolution in January 2011. The expanding blogging community had already undermined the credibility of state media, long before the 2011 revolution, by exposing the lies spread by state-owned media, on behalf of Mubarak's regime, and offering an alternative more credible source of news.

By the beginning of 2011, the Khaled Said page on Facebook called for organizing nation-wide protests against police brutality on January 25th, the Police Anniversary Day. The protests goal was to challenge police repression and call for an end to the state of emergency and the systematic torture of civilians.[70] The success of the Tunisian Revolution, on January 14th, in bringing down Ben Ali's dictatorship encouraged activists in Egypt to see the planned anti-police protests on January 25th as a potential spark for an anti-regime revolution. As the nonviolent protests succeeded in building and keeping momentum for three consecutive days, the international community started to call it a revolution and Mubarak's regime started to feel threatened. Ironically, Mubarak tried to block Internet service on the third day of the protests to distract protesters and block the news coming via bloggers from Tahrir Square. However, the lack of credibility of state-owned media caused the regime's move to block the internet to backfire against him, rather than disturb the momentum of the revolution. The inability of families' elders to communicate with their young members, who were participating in the protests, compelled parents to go to the focal points of protest to check on their children. As soon as they got there and directly witnessed the nonviolent protests, they decided to join. Motivated by anger over police brutality, inspired by the success of Tunisians in toppling their dictator, and highly committed to nonviolent discipline, the January 25th protesters brought down Mubarak within only eighteen days.

The Unique Dynamics of Revolution 2011:

The uniqueness of Egypt's revolution lies in the fact that, for the most part, the eighteen days of protests constituted a rare nonviolent combat between two nonviolent blocs: the protesters, who were committed to being nonviolent from the very beginning, and the military forces, who unexpectedly chose to put aside their traditional weapons and employ *"reverse nonviolent action"* to contain the protesters. Gene Sharp assigned four mechanisms that guarantees the success of a nonviolent movement in conflicting with a powerful and violent opponent, they are: accommodation, conversion, coercion, and disintegration.[71] In Egypt's 2011 revolution, those four mechanisms were cleverly applied by the young leaders of the revolution, who received training on those specific tactics in the US and Europe, earlier. Yet, it was surprising how the military forces strategically chose to respond by employing the same four nonviolent tactics to contain protesters and control the outcomes of the revolution. That is what this research describes as *"reverse nonviolent action"* and introduces to scholars as a whole new theory in the field of studying nonviolent action and strategy.

Dalia Ziada

The dynamics of the nonviolent conflict between the protesters and the military, which led to the eventual success of the 2011 revolution, can best be explained through understanding the power relations between the people, Mubarak, and Mubarak's mightiest pillars of support: the military and the police forces.

Mubarak was not only a former military aviator and the Commander of Air Forces, during the 1973 war against Israel. According to the working constitution, at that time, and the military law, in application since 1952 revolution, the President of the State acts as the Supreme Leader of the Armed Forces. In other words, Mubarak remained a military commander till his last day in power. His legacy and popularity was heavily dependent on his history of achievements as an officer in the armed forces. Over the course of his Presidency, Mubarak gradually minimized the role of the military in public life, but without diminishing or withdrawing any of their powers and privileges. Talking about the affairs of the military institution was considered a "red line" that local media outlets were not allowed to cross. No one was allowed to discuss or comment on the Armed Forces' budget, size, or extent of power. Under Mubarak's illiberal democratic style of governance, the military played a clear role in keeping political and economic developments under control, without necessarily interfering in the day-to-day policy making process. The Egyptian military was, sporadically, commissioned to handle non-traditional missions, such as providing humanitarian aid to grassroots citizens during times of natural disasters or economic crises. Two major incidents that solidified the positive relationship between the people and the military during the Mubarak era were: military's intervention to rescue victims of the earthquake in October 1992, and military's offering affordable quality bread for grassroots citizens during the bread crisis in 2008.[72]

In parallel, Mubarak established a symbiotic relationship with the police forces, who gradually changed their priorities from maintaining order through serving the public, into assaulting citizens to protect the state. As soon as Mubarak was automatically upgraded to the position of the President of the State, after Sadat's assassination in 1981, he instated the state of emergency, purportedly to deal with the Islamic extremists responsible for the assassination of Sadat.[73] The state of emergency gave police forces cover for the mistreatment of civilians, unjustified arrests, torture, and detention without declaring charges. In the 1990s, with the rise of violent Jihadist movements that executed various terrorist attacks in Cairo and Upper Egypt, the police forces were given a *carte blanche* to become more brutal in dealing with suspects. By the emergence of the nonviolent movement in 2004, the police forces were instructed to deal with the political dissidents. Police's State Security Department was trained to deal with terrorists and was not prepared to handle political nonviolent dissidents.[74] They used extreme violence against nonviolent protesters, harassed bloggers and journalists, closed human rights NGOs, and threatened liberal democratic activists. The brutality of police forces against the activists and ordinary citizens damaged the relationship between the people and the police forces. The killing of Khaled Said in Alexandria by two policemen was the tipping point of this relationship of hatred and fear between the people and police forces. Indeed, the January 25th revolution was initially planned as a protest on police brutality on the police anniversary day.[75]

Disintegrating Repressive Police Forces:

It took the nonviolent protesters of 2011 revolution only four days to force the police forces to suspend their operations. In dealing with police forces, the nonviolent protesters used three of Gene Sharp's four mechanisms: conversion, disintegration, and coercion.

The protesters, first, tried to convert the young police personnel, who were commissioned by higher rank policemen to surround the protesters into tight circles, beat them with sticks, and disperse them with tear gas bombs. According to George Lakey, conversion means "the opponent, as the result of the actions of the nonviolent struggle group or person, comes around to a new point of view which embraces the ends of the nonviolent actor."[76]

The nonviolent protesters thought it would be easy to convert the police personnel through creating mutual understanding and empathy with them. They responded to their violent assaults with offering food and water and speaking to them about the legitimacy of the protests. However, as Gene Sharp noted, conversion is the tactic with the highest potential for failure, because it is impractical in most cases and depends on a number of factors that makes it too complicated to work effectively. "The factors influencing conversion include the degree of conflict of interest and the social distance between the contending groups, the personalities of the opponents, shared or contrasting beliefs and norms between the groups, and the role of third parties... for various reasons, including unsatisfactory fulfillment of the above influential factors, conversion efforts may only partially succeed or may fail completely."[77] In fact, protesters' attempts to convert policemen did not work because soldiers' fear of punishment if they disobeyed their commanding officers was greater than their empathy towards the protesters and understanding of the cause of the protests.

Therefore, the nonviolent protesters decided to try another tactic; i.e. disintegration. Usually, disintegration is implemented as an advanced step toward nonviolent coercion. According to Sharp; "in nonviolent coercion, the opponents are not converted, nor do they decide to accommodate to the demands. Rather, shifts of social forces and power relationships produce the changes sought by the resisters against the will of the opponents... The concept of disintegration takes the process one step further... so that the opponent group falls completely apart. No coherent body remains capable even of accepting defeat."[78] Hence, the protesters attempted to coerce the police forces by organizing simultaneous massive rallies and sit-ins at several locations all over Egypt, with preserving strict commitment to nonviolent discipline. As a result, the police forces were effectively disintegrated as they failed, due to their limited number and equipment, to control the simultaneous and widely spread demonstrations. At the same time, protesters' commitment to nonviolent discipline undermined the legitimacy of the police's violent attacks on nonviolent unarmed activists. The disintegration of the police forces put Mubarak's regime under huge pressure, and paralyzed the daily routine activities of the government, which eventually resulted in motivating government employees to join the protests.

On the fourth day of the revolution, January 28th, the police received orders from the military to leave all main squares, as the military forces were warming up to deal directly with the protests. The tattered relationship between public citizens and police forces, and the urgency to end police repression, overwhelmed citizens' fear of escaping prisoners, after police's disintegration. Rather than begging for police forces to return to work, people organized themselves to defend their houses against any potential attacks by escaping prisoners who broke out of prison during revolution time, while making sure not to disturb the flow of the revolution in Tahrir Square and other focal points in different cities.

Confusions about the Nonviolent Military:

The hard-won victory of nonviolent protesters over the violent police forces was not enough to bring Mubarak down, as he continued to rely on a stronger pillar of support - the military forces. The military, also known as the Armed Forces, was sent to contain and end the revolution on the evening of the 28th of January, a few hours after the police received orders to withdraw from main squares. The next fourteen days marked an intense nonviolent battle between the protesters and the army's leadership. Apparently, the military learned from the tragic defeat of the police forces and decided not to use violence against the protesters and rather adopted the nonviolent tactics of conversion and accommodation – much like their opposition – while staying on the fence in terms of abandoning Mubarak.

Dalia Ziada

Egypt's case is, allegedly, the first case in history in which a military puts aside their traditional weapons and use nonviolent tactics to contain and end a nonviolent revolution. In some instances of successful nonviolent uprisings – e.g. in Philippines 1986, Ukraine 2004, and Tunisia 2010 – the military refrained from using violence against protesters. Yet, the active participation of the Egyptian military in the nonviolent conflict is what makes the case of Egypt's revolution the first in the history of nonviolent action. In other words, the Egyptian military did not only choose not to kill the people, but also made the strategic decision to use *"reverse nonviolent action"* to contain the nonviolent protesters and direct the outcomes of the revolution.

The military first appeared in Tahrir Square in Cairo, Suez, and Alexandria on the night of January 28th; a few hours after the police forces were defeated and withdrew. According to eyewitnesses at Tahrir Square, including the writer of this book, there was a strong feeling of caution when the military tanks descended from Kasr El-

The Curious Case of the Three-Legged Wolf

Nile Bridge heading towards Tahrir Square and State TV Building. "Some people expected the tanks are coming to kill us, and everyone was asking what should we do about it," one of the protesters outside State TV Building at that night mentioned.[79] "Almost everyone agreed to stand still and continue the fight till the end." After a few moments of wary silence, "some protesters rushed in front of the first tank shouting 'God is great' making it clear that any further forward movement would be over shattered bodies."[80] A few moments later, an unknown voice among protesters chanted the slogan that has become the icon of the revolution since then: "the people and the army are one hand!" Protesters repeated the chant until a collective sense of confidence developed and peoples' fear evaporated.[81] According to eyewitnesses from Suez, similar slogans were chanted there too, but no one knows who started them. It is rumored that the military sent a soldier in civil clothes to hide among the protesters and chant the slogan "the people and the army are one hand" at the moment of the arrival of the troops. There is no evidence either way about the origins of the slogan. However, this was exactly the same slogan chanted at the 1952 revolution, which empowered the military to rule the country, after dethroning the King.[82] Apparently, this was the first successful nonviolent tactic used by the military to convert the nonviolent protesters from opposition into allies.

As both protestors and the military were engaging in strategies of conversion, by signaling the potential of cooperation and solidarity with one another, strong emotions of empathy were created among the protesters and the military soldiers and young officers, who were sent to control the revolution. The long positive relationship between the people and the military and the lack of any apparent conflict of interests between them were important factors that helped the military succeed in employing the tactic of conversion against protesters. Meanwhile, the narrowness of the social and age gap between the two groups increased the potential of converting the young officers into revolutionaries. In fact, the April 8th Movement of Military Officers,[83] which

The Curious Case of the Three-Legged Wolf

appeared after the fall of Mubarak to rebel against elder military leaders, was formed by some of these young officers. Eventually, the military succeeded in converting the people into their supporters, but only partially.

Despite conversion, the protesters were able to maintain the momentum of the revolution by continuing the nation-wide rallies and protests calling for the end of Mubarak's presidency. While some protesters chanted, "people and the army are one hand," their colleagues were chanting "people want Mubarak down." The military chose to accommodate the resistance movement by pressuring Mubarak to offer some concessions to the protesters, including: dissolving the ministerial cabinet and government, hiring a vice president, pledging that he would leave office at the end of his term in 2011, and ensuring that his son, Gamal, would not run for presidency. Even more, the military pressured Mubarak to give away one of his secondary pillars of support by dissolving the National Democratic Party and annulling the results of the 2010 parliamentary elections.

Accommodation after conversion was an effective mechanism of success for the military in the nonviolent conflict with protesters. According to Sharp; "in accommodation, the opponents are neither converted nor nonviolently coerced. The opponents, without having changed their minds fundamentally about the issues involved, resolve to grant at least some of the demands of the nonviolent resisters."[84] The ability of nonviolent activists to persist despite the repression by police, played an important role in military leaders' decisions to accommodate the movement, but the motives behind the military's pressuring Mubarak to yield to the demands of the people were not limited to the direct pressure of the massive protests. Most likely, the military chose to accommodate as part of a strategy that Gene Sharp describes as "adjusting to opposition within their own group, and acting to prevent the growth of that opposition."[85] By choosing to accommodate, the Supreme Council of Armed Forces (SCAF), succeeded in controlling potential dissidence inside the military structure, and winning more legitimacy among the people that helped generate more supporters for the military's actions, later.

Mubarak's Fall into Prisoner's Dilemma:

While the military got busy with applying reverse nonviolent tactics to engage protesters, Mubarak appeared to feel abandoned. He agreed to yield to the military's pressure and offered a number of concessions, but the protesters still insisted on removing him from power. The more concessions he offered, the more legitimacy he lost, and the more legitimacy the military won. Apparently, the heated nonviolent conflict between the protesters and the military affected the quality of communication between the military generals and the regime. Mubarak could not understand why the military disobeyed his orders to shoot the protesters and instead preferred to contain the situation using reverse nonviolent tactics. The fear of being abandoned by his own military generals pushed Mubarak to fall in the trap of prisoner's dilemma.[86] Fearing that the military was double-crossing him, Mubarak started to make decisions that threatened the high-profile military leaders, including the Minister of Defense and SCAF generals.

On February 2nd, Mubarak ordered the leaders of the dissolved NDP to incite the owners of tourist camels and horses from the Pyramids area to carry swords and go to finish protesters in Tahrir Square.[87] Mubarak was planning to scare protesters out of Tahrir Square and provoke suspicions against the military and the new Prime Minister, Ahmed Shafiq, who promised no protester would be hurt.[88] This uncalculated move by Mubarak backfired against him, as it strengthened the relationship between the military and protesters, who together fought against the armed riders of the camels and horses. At the same time, it aroused the suspicions of SCAF leaders that Mubarak was trying to discredit them among the protesters. Consequently, SCAF decided to stop informing Mubarak about their plans and began to adopt a policy of neutrality towards the regime. This made Mubarak more suspicious of the intentions of SCAF and widened the rift between him and SCAF generals.[89] The protesters' determination to bring

The Curious Case of the Three-Legged Wolf

down Mubarak escalated after the Camels and Horses Battle. As the military adopted a position of neutrality, it became easier for the nonviolent movement to attract the military to their side. At the same time, the military was more interested in attracting protesters to its side out of fear of being deposed along with Mubarak.

On February 9th, Mubarak made the mistake that turned his last standing friends into foes. He sent a disc to State Television including a video for immediate release. In the video, Mubarak recorded his decision to remove General Tantawy, the Minister of Defense, the highest-ranking officer in SCAF, and one of Mubarak's most loyal associates. The Director of News Sector at State Television was shocked when he watched the video and immediately called SCAF leaders to inform them about it. After consulting with General Tantawy, General Etman, the Director of Morale Affairs Department of the Egyptian Military, at that time, asked State Television to broadcast another video that shows the Supreme Council of Armed Forces (SCAF) being convened for the first time without

Mubarak.[90] Thirty-eight hours later, Omar Suleiman, Mubarak's Vice President and Director of General Intelligence Department, appeared on State Television to announce Mubarak's resignation and decision to transfer political power to SCAF.[91] Due to military's success in applying reverse nonviolent tactics of conversion and accommodation, earlier, the people embraced Mubarak's transfer of political power to the military. Even, the members of the Muslim Brotherhood, who ideologically reject the rule of the military, were compelled to accommodate and accept the new statuesque.

The Foreign Affairs Role in 2011 Revolution:

According to the majority of Arab Spring scholarship, the motives behind SCAF leadership decision to abandon Mubarak and side with the nonviolent protesters could be summarized in the following four propositions:

The Curious Case of the Three-Legged Wolf

1. The military abandoned Mubarak because the military leaders had a personal interest in undermining Mubarak's plans to groom his son Gamal for the presidency because some rejected hereditary system and thought Gamal's economic power, as a civilian, would threaten the officers' interests, so they chose to take advantage of the revolution to achieve that goal;

2. The military is an independent institution, and it is not necessarily dependent on Mubarak's patronage. The military chose to abandon Mubarak to preserve their legitimacy and their power on one hand and keeping the well-being of the state on the other hand;

3. The decision to disobey Mubarak's orders to kill the protesters was motivated by international pressure, especially from the friends of the Egyptian military in the US military; and

4. The positive historical relationship between the military officers and the people made it harder for the military to kill the people and easier to disobey Mubarak.

The third proposition holds that the military's decision not to shoot the protesters was motivated by their allies in the US Army. The Egyptian and the American military have long maintained strong relationships. Since the peace agreement with Israel in 1970s, the US has been committed to providing a huge annual aid of 1.3 billion dollars to the Egyptian military.[92] The second proposition on the independence of the military institution helps explain why there was international interest in communicating directly with the SCAF leaders rather than contacting Mubarak after the military got involved in containing the protests on January 28th. The Egyptian military sends young and mid-rank officers to the US to receive trainings on warfare, as well as on civil issues, such as human rights, democracy, peace, and non-traditional roles of the military in non-war times.[93] The older higher-ranking officers used to travel to the United States once every year to meet with military leaders at the Pentagon. When the revolution erupted in January 2011, the Egyptian Minister of Defense, the Army Chief of Staff, and generals from SCAF were in the US for their annual meeting with Pentagon leaders. They had to cut their visit short and return to Egypt on January 27th, to deal with the revolution.

In an interview with the US Joint Staff Spokesperson, he noted that "General Sami Anan and a military delegation were in Washington, DC for the US-Egypt annual Military Cooperation Commission meetings in January 2011. These meetings aimed to advance the peace and security of both nations by discussing security assistance, military training, and industrial defense cooperation. Meetings of this kind are a routine part of the long-standing military-to-military relationship of the United States and Egypt."[94] He explained further that when the protests erupted in Egypt, the Egyptian military leaders discussed the issue with their US military counterparts before ending the meeting to go back to Egypt. According to the Joint Staff Spokesperson, "the US military leaders discussed a number of topics with Egyptian military leaders in this meeting to include the political-military situation in Egypt. Although, it would not be appropriate to discuss the details of those conversations, the US military, to include the Chairman of the Joint Chiefs of Staff (at the time) Admiral Mike Mullen, publically and repeatedly encouraged the Egyptian military to refrain from violence against the protesters and commended them on their professionalism and restraint."[95] Although the US military urged the leaders of the Egyptian army to refrain from killing the protesters and encouraged them to use nonviolent tactics to contain the situation, they emphasized that the army should not let Mubarak down. "Although, we heard suggestions that the military was committed at first to remaining loyal to Mubarak, unlike the Tunisian military, which defected from Ben Ali." Moreover, the US Joint Staff Spokesperson said to me, "I can tell you that at no point did the US advocate the overthrow of President Mubarak but rather emphasized the need for genuine change to meet the demands of the protestors and expressed the confidence the US had in the Egyptian military to see Egypt through its governmental transition."[96] Indeed, US support for the Egyptian military is consistent, regardless who is the president of the state. This attitude provided the military with latitude to side with the protesters rather than protecting Mubarak regime. In addition, "the fact that the Egyptian army is a conscript force drawn from all segments of society also seems to have contributed to its identification with demands of the protesters."[97] The power relationship between the people and the military versus the power relationship between the military and the regime made it easier for the military to choose to align with the protesters.

Chapter 5
From Mubarak's Super Long Autocracy to Muslim Brotherhood's Super Short Theocracy

"If it is not me, it is the Muslim Brotherhood," said Mubarak in almost every media appearance he made or diplomatic meeting he convened.[98] Indeed, the liberal democratic activists, who brought down Mubarak's three decades of dictatorship, by a nonviolent revolution in 2011, did not realize that they were paving the way for the Muslim Brotherhood to achieve their long-awaited dream to rule Egypt, and apply Islamic Sharia as a political system of governance.[99] Ironically, the Muslim Brotherhood used to assure young liberal activists that the group does not seek political power, claiming that the group's one and only goal is Da'wa; i.e. to freely practice and preach their version of Islamism to the general public.[100] On the ground, the Muslim Brotherhood's manipulative actions were

completely contradictory to their idealist discourse. Although they had never encouraged the revolution against Mubarak, but they worked strategically to take advantage of the revolution's success in a way that allowed them to eventually take over the presidency of the state and the ultimate majority of the parliament, by mid-2012.

How did the Muslim Brotherhood hijack the 2011 Revolution?

In their quest to the mountaintop of political power in Egypt, the Muslim Brotherhood applied a number of nonviolent tactics against:

(1) the liberal democratic activists, who initiated the revolution;

(2) the Supreme Council of Armed Forces (SCAF), which took over Egypt's political leadership after the fall of Mubarak, and

(3) Al-Azhar's Grand Imam, Ahmed Al-Tayeb, their old foe, whom they counted as a serious threat to their agenda to apply Islamic Sharia.

Tactic 1: Neutralizing liberal activists:

The Muslim Brotherhood did not participate in the nonviolent protests that led to the 2011 revolution. They neither planned nor initiated any of the rallies that called for Mubarak's removal, during the first week of the revolution. Instead, the Muslim Brotherhood leaders spoke publicly against activists' calls for protesting on police anniversary. However, after one week of successful continuous protests, the Muslim Brotherhood leaders decided to send their young members to streets to join other revolutionists, without declaring their collective identity as members of the Muslim Brotherhood. They did not use any specific Muslim Brotherhood logos or Islamic slogans, but they moved together in blocs. Meanwhile, the

The Curious Case of the Three-Legged Wolf

leaders of the group started to make media statements praising the revolution and echoing activists call for ousting Mubarak.[101] At the beginning, the members of the Muslim Brotherhood were not welcomed by liberal revolutionists, who resented their decline to participate in the January 25th protests from the beginning. However, this resentment vanished when the highly organized youth of the Muslim Brotherhood managed to defend the scattered nonviolent protesters against one of Mubarak's attempts to disperse the protests in Tahrir Square.

On February 2nd, members of Mubarak's dissolved National Democratic Party (NDP) paid owners of tourist camels and horses around the Pyramids area in Giza, to storm into Tahrir Square riding their camels and horses and walk over the bodies of the sitting-in protesters.[102] As helpless as nonviolent liberal activists were, the camels attack was supposed to succeed in scaring and scattering the activists' gatherings. However, the presence of the Muslim Brotherhood youth, who recently joined the protests, altered the whole scenario in favor of the revolutionists. When the camel riders stormed into Tahrir square, the participating youth of the Muslim Brotherhood, used the martial combat skills they acquired through the group's secret militia training, to counter the attack. In a few seconds, they organized themselves into "U" shape around the helpless and shocked protesters to protect them. Meanwhile, the front liners pulled the attackers off of their camels and horses and combated them. This specific scene ignited a strong bond of sympathy and trust between the young liberal protesters and the youth of the Muslim Brotherhood. As their popularity grew among protesters, the Muslim Brotherhood leaders started presenting themselves to foreign media as spokespersons of the revolution. They also stepped up to negotiate, on behalf of the protesters, with Mubarak's regime and intelligence. The politically inexperienced and naively idealist young liberal activists were too occupied by their anger against Mubarak's regime to plan for the next steps after the fall of the dictator. Their lack of organization and clear long-term vision was a point of weakness, which the highly organized and politically skilled Muslim Brotherhood manipulated to hijack the revolution.

The leaders of the Muslim Brotherhood took advantage of the successful integration of their young members into the protests to deceive the international community into believing that Egypt is going through an "Islamic revolution." This myth was quickly busted by a poll, which the Washington Institute for Near East Studies conducted in early February 2011, on the nature and motives of the Egyptians protesting against Mubarak.[103] The poll was taken by phone calls in the midst of the upheaval. The final results indicated that the 2011 uprising was not an Islamic revolution. The Muslim Brotherhood was approved by just fifteen per cent of surveyed Egyptians and its leaders got barely one per cent of the vote in a presidential straw poll. Asked to pick national priorities, only twelve per cent of surveyed Egyptians chose Islamic Sharia law over Egypt's regional leadership, democracy, or economic development. And, when asked to explain the uprising's motives, the surveyed sample selected econc conditions, corruption, and unemployment (around thirty per cent each), which far outpaced the concern that "the regime is not Islamic enough" (only seven per cent). Yet, this did not stop policy-makers in Washington from supporting the Muslim Brotherhood as an alternative to Mubarak.[104]

Tactic 2: Discrediting military as a political leader:

After neutralizing the liberal democratic youth, Muslim Brotherhood's next challenge was the highly popular military. The Egyptian military was not only popular among the Egyptian people, but also for Egypt's most powerful ally, the United States. The strong ties between Egyptian and American military helped shape a lot of vital decisions in Egypt's domestic policies, regional geo-politics, and diplomatic affairs, since the reign of Sadat. After the fall of Mubarak, The Supreme Council of Armed Forces (SCAF) was assigned as the political transitional ruler of the country. The people, including young liberal revolutionists, did not oppose handing power, temporarily, to SCAF until

The Curious Case of the Three-Legged Wolf

a new constitution and presidential elections be convened. In general, the military is highly respected and trusted by the public citizens. In addition, the military played a very important role in making the revolution succeed by declining to use violence against the protesters. Yet, the Muslim Brotherhood felt threatened by this increasing popularity of the military. Therefore, their next challenge was to destroy military's credibility in the eyes of the Egyptian public and Egypt's Western allies.

Accordingly, the Muslim Brotherhood built on the momentum of the successful revolution to keep nonviolent protests in the streets going for longer. This way, they managed to keep SCAF busy with trying to control chaos at home, while enhancing the mostly-false impression inherited by Egypt's Western allies, especially the United States of America, that the Egyptian people collectively rejected military's political rule. This was necessary so the Muslim Brotherhood can introduce their group to the world as the best potential alternative to Mubarak's regime. In parallel, the ongoing protests were an excellent opportunity for the Muslim Brotherhood leaders to engage with public citizens and promote their Islamic Sharia agenda to them, as an alternative to Mubarak's secular and corrupt government. While Muslim Brotherhood efforts to discredit the military gained momentum at home and abroad, high profile members of the Muslim Brotherhood, such as the group's spiritual leader Yusuf Al-Qaradawi, were invited to speak to the public at Tahrir Square about the political applications of Islamic Sharia.[105]

Every Friday, in Tahrir Square, the Muslim Brotherhood organized and led a massive protest. On the first two Friday protests, they were celebrating the success of the revolution alongside liberal democratic activists and ordinary non-politicized citizens. Later on, the Muslim Brotherhood started to invite other social categories into the protests to call for their economic rights, including the members of disadvantaged trade unions. Gradually, after about two months of regular Friday protests, the Muslim Brotherhood members and leaders started to openly attack the military leadership and criticize almost all SCAF decisions and moves. On one of those protests against the military, the Muslim Brotherhood brought to square some young military officers, in military uniform, who announced their rebellion against SCAF, which is loaded with much older military commanders.[106] The young officers claimed that the army is a corrupt institution and that people should rebel against it. Since then, the slogan "down with military rule" became a stable in all the Friday protests that happened afterward. This was the first indication on Muslim Brotherhood's success in damaging military's popularity and reputation among local citizens and Western allies. Soon after, the Muslim Brotherhood officially revealed their plans to run for presidency and parliament.

Tactic 3: Overthrowing Al-Azhar's Samurai; Ahmed Al-Tayeb:

After neutralizing revolutionists, especially the super idealist liberal democrats, and discrediting the military domestically and internationally, the next challenge for the Muslim Brotherhood, in their quest to power, was abolishing Ahmed Al-Tayeb, the Grand Imam of Al-Azhar. Al-Tayeb has always been a thorn in the back of the Muslim Brotherhood, since he was a professor at Al-Azhar University. Muslim Brotherhood leaders knew that they could not promote their extremist agenda of governing through Islamic Sharia, while he continued in commanding Al-Azhar; the most credible Muslim scholarly institution in the entire world. They could not think of dismantling Al-Azhar, as an institution, because this should have had ignited anger against the group by its religious grassroots supporters. At the same time, they did not want Western allies to see the Muslim Brotherhood as an Islamic group fighting moderate Islam, represented in Al-Tayeb as the Grand Imam, and in Al-Azhar as a worldly renowned centrist Muslim institution.

Therefore, the Muslim Brotherhood resorted to nonviolent action, once more, to pressure for overthrowing Al-Tayeb from the leadership of Al-Azhar. The Muslim Brotherhood affiliated students at Al-Azhar University,

The Curious Case of the Three-Legged Wolf

instructed by Muslim Brotherhood leaders, organized a series of complaint-based protests inside the university's campus, about internal administrative policies related to students' fees, employees' rights, teachers' salaries, etc. As the protests inside the campus succeeded in gaining momentum and higher number of supporters, the Muslim Brotherhood organized much louder and wider protests outside the office of Dr. Ahmed Al-Tayeb at the headquarters of the Sheikhdom of Al-Azhar. The biggest of those protests took place on the 26th of April, 2011.[107] More than fifteen thousand scholars, employees, teachers and students from Al-Azhar gathered outside the office of Al-Tayeb calling for Al-Azhar's legal independence from state and for electing a new Grand Imam.

In a stubborn response that shocked and confused the Muslim Brotherhood, Al-Tayeb refused to resign and decided to fight back. He made a public statement indicating that his resignation would put Al-Azhar in the hands of the "wrong people," in reference to religiously extremist professors affiliated to the Muslim

Brotherhood and the Salafist movement. He asserted that "as a servant of Islam and a servant of Al-Azhar," he would stand strong in the face of the protests, while continue to exert his best efforts to improve Al-Azhar's governance system and educational curricula.[108] The following day, Al-Tayeb announced the launch of an initiative, under his direct supervision, to "reform Al-Azhar" from within, which he described to media as the "best response to the protests calling for Al-Azhar's independence."[109] The initiative included working on: (1) forming a legal committee to review and suggest amendments to Al-Azhar's Law no. 103 of 1961, to seek Al-Azhar's independence from the political power of the state; (2) setting new regulations for the process of electing and appointing the Grand Imam by the Council of Senior Scholars; and (3) composing an academic committee to review and modify the educational curricula of Al-Azhar University. The initiative was widely welcomed by Al-Azhar scholars, as well as political observers, in Egypt and abroad.

The Curious Case of the Three-Legged Wolf

Immediately after the launch of the initiative to reform Al-Azhar from within, Al-Tayeb decided to actively participate in managing the political chaos that took place in the aftermath of the 2011 revolution. He was, perhaps, motivated by the fact that this chaos was enabling extremists from the Muslim Brotherhood and the Salafists and, thus, became a threat to Al-Azhar and moderate Islam. "Since 2011 Revolution, as Egypt's political elite became apparently increasingly bogged down in seemingly endless feuds over the Islamist versus liberal identity of post-revolutionary Egypt, Al-Azhar has emerged as the only universally respected institution capable of bringing about national unity, or at least dialogue, among the different views."[110] Between June and August 2011, Al-Tayeb organized and led six meetings and negotiations between political competitors and intellectuals, to discuss the political future of Egypt.[111] Those meetings played a tremendous role in avoiding violent clashes between competing political parties, and also contributed to downsizing street protests, as political parties and movements did not need to go to the streets to manage their conflicts, anymore. Meanwhile, those meetings re-profiled Al-Tayeb in a new light for the general public as not only a highly respected religious leader but also as a powerful political mastermind. This qualified Al-Tayeb to win the respect and admiration of SCAF generals, who viewed him as a patriot ally and an unbeatable fighter against the Muslim Brotherhood.

As the Muslim Brotherhood lost hope in overthrowing the "Samurai" of Al-Azhar, the Grand Imam Dr. Ahmed Al-Tayeb, they focused more on manipulating the religious piety of the grassroots citizens to control the parliament. By the end of 2011, the Muslim Brotherhood and their Salafist allies won the majority of parliament seats, and thus seized control over Egypt's legislative power. In anticipation to their attempts to amend Al-Azhar laws and oust Al-Tayeb from the position of the Grand Imam, the Supreme Council of Armed Forces (SCAF) stepped up to protect Al-Azhar and Al-Tayeb. The new members of parliament, mostly Islamist affiliates of the Muslim

The Curious Case of the Three-Legged Wolf

Brotherhood and the Salafist Movement, were planned to swear in on the 23rd of January, 2012. On the 19th of January, SCAF issued Decree no. 13 of 2012 granting Al-Azhar independence from the political state and preserving the current Grand Imam, Ahmed Al-Tayeb, in his position with immunity against removal by the political government of the state. In addition, the decree stipulated the Grand Imam's complete control, in consultation with the Council of Senior Scholars, over all internal affairs related to Al-Azhar and its affiliated religious, educational, and research facilities.[112] In December 2012, a new constitution was composed by a specialized committee of representatives of all political powers and respective government institutions. Article 4 of the new constitution armored the privileges given to Al-Azhar and Al-Tayeb in SCAF's Decree no. 13 of 2012.[113]

    Eventually, Al-Tayeb won another episode in his personal and professional long battle against the Muslim Brotherhood and the Salafists. It is remarkable that despite the political and legislative powers the Muslim Brotherhood possessed, at that time, they could not twist Al-Tayeb's arm or control Al-Azhar. One can, contentedly, claim that Al-Tayeb's iron stance, supported by the military leadership, against the expansion of political Islamists over Al-Azhar, saved Egypt from becoming a hub for the violent jihadists messing around with the Middle East region.

Islamists' Extremely Disappointing One Year in Power:

On the 24th of June 2012, the Muslim Brotherhood candidate, Mohamed Morsi, was announced as the new president of Egypt. He won elections with a very narrow margin (51.7%) against Mubarak's former prime minister and former military Aviator General, Ahmed Shafik.[114] Morsi's victory was widely celebrated by Western media, academia, and political observers, as a step towards containing Islamic extremism within an organized political system. However, the general reaction in Egypt was a heightened sense of shock and defeat, especially among the liberal democratic activists, who initiated the revolution.[115] Indeed, Egyptians wanted to end Mubarak's super long three decades of autocracy. But the majority of Egyptians, who participated in the revolution against Mubarak, had never wanted or expected to see Egypt turning into an Islamist theocracy governed by the Muslim Brotherhood in presidency and the Salafists in parliament.[116] Several non-governmental organizations that were monitoring the electoral process, then, collected evidence on forgery and fraud that took place in favor of Morsi.[117] However, the rise of Islamists to the top of political and legislative powers, in 2012, was not challenged by any one. The military and the liberal democrats had no choice but to swallow their defeat and accept the new statuesque, though with much bitterness and resentment. Should the military challenged the ascendance of Islamists to presidential and legislative powers, Egypt would have been exposed to a huge national security threat. Legitimately, military's worst fear, during the aftermath of the 2011 revolution, was to see Egypt "turning into another Syria or Libya" drowning under bloody chapters of infinite civil wars.[118] On the other hand, the liberal democrat's worst fear was to see Egypt retouring back to being a dictatorship under one of Mubarak's political associates, in case they opposed or challenged the results of the elections.[119]

Nevertheless, the rise of Islamists in politics marked a turning point in the whole dynamic of political interactions between the Islamists, liberal democratic activists, and the military. That was also the beginning of a whole new chapter on the way the average citizens viewed the legitimacy of the revolution, the viability of democratization, and the effectiveness of political participation, in general. Furthermore, the majority of Egyptian citizens, pushed by fear of losing their unique and complex Egyptian identity to Islamization and governance through Islamic Sharia, chose to quietly retreat to their safe caves of apathy and watch the unfolding political developments on television screens from the comfort of their homes. A new term called "the Couch Party" was heavily used by media and analysts, at that time, to describe the phenomenon.[120] Ironically, the Muslim

Brotherhood did not care to relieve the public's fear, to console the defeated liberal democrats, or even to negotiate a working deal with the military generals. On the contrary, the Salafists in parliament and the Muslim Brotherhood in presidency took every wrong step towards alienating themselves and arousing political and popular anger against their regime.

First, the Muslim Brotherhood turned against the military generals. On the first week of August 2012, nearly one month after Muslim Brotherhood's Mohamed Morsi was seated as president, Morsi fired the two most popular leaders of the Armed Forces: Field Marshal Mohammed Tantawy, the Minister of Defense and his Army Chief of Staff, General Sami Anan.[121] Together, Tantawy and Anan had complete control over the military for decades. Both commanders were highly respected by the Egyptian public and military leaders at Middle Eastern and Western countries with close ties to Egypt; including Israel, the United States, France, and Russia. Ironically, what the Muslim Brotherhood thought was a "bold" act to control the military institution, turned out, later, to be their most injudicious decision. The new Minister of Defense, Abdel Fattah Al-Sisi, appointed by Morsi after the removal of Tantawy played a tremendous role in supporting the Egyptian people's uprising against the Muslim Brotherhood, ten months later, in June 2013.

In parliament, the performance of Salafists was not only shocking to the public citizens, but also threatening to the liberal and democratic values that the young people embraced throughout the 2011 revolution. The legislations discussed by Islamist Members of Parliament were not about improving economy or advancing democracy. Rather, the Islamist Members of Parliament were pre-occupied by making new laws to legalize Female Genital Mutilation and prevent women from working in certain fields that they believed should be reserved exclusively to men.[122] Yet, the most shocking behavior by Islamist parliamentarians was when they refused to stand up to honor the Egyptian national anthem, claiming that this is a non-Islamic practice.[123] Even worse, some Salafist

The Curious Case of the Three-Legged Wolf

Members of Parliament used to disrespectfully disturb parliamentary discussions by standing up without permission and loudly reciting the Islamic "Azan" (the call for prayer), and then leaving the open parliamentary session to perform prayer.[124]

A few days before the runoff elections that brought the Muslim Brotherhood's Morsi to presidency, the Muslim Brotherhood invited professionals from human rights nongovernmental organizations to meet with the leaders of the group.[125] After the long speech blurted by Muslim Brotherhood's leaders about their willingness to empower civil society organizations and respect human rights, a participating human rights activist raised his hand to ask a question. "I saw in your booklet that you value human rights and women's rights in compliance with Islamic Sharia," he asked. "Are those Islamic human and women's rights similar to the rights stipulated in the international conventions and declarations of the United Nations, which the group usually denounces?" The answer given by one of Morsi's advisers was appalling. "Islamic Sharia values women's rights more than the international conventions do," the Morsi adviser said. "Do you know that according to Islamic Sharia, the woman may choose not to breastfeed her child or clean the house until her husband pays her for doing this?" he added confidently to much shock and laughter in the room. The Muslim Brotherhood and their Salafist allies had always kept women within a frame of biological stereotypes as a mother, child-bearer, and housewife. Along their history, Muslim Brotherhood leaders described women's rights as a foreign set of western values.[126] The space provided for women on the Brotherhood's official website, for instance, was called "Family Oasis" and was filled with skill-sharing articles about bringing up children, serving and pleasing one's husband, and the modest dress code for Muslim woman. Within the group's hierarchy, the Muslim Brotherhood had a shameful record of marginalizing women. The "Muslim Sisters" branch inside the Muslim Brotherhood had never been allowed access to leadership positions inside the group.[127]

The Curious Case of the Three-Legged Wolf

The Muslim Brotherhood changed this discriminative policy towards women, only after establishing their political party, in the months following the 2011 revolution. To complement their political ambitions, the party hired a few women in its supreme committee, so they appear as liberal and open-minded to Western observers. Those women were, in fact, the wives and daughters of the leaders of the group. They had zero record of political activism to be qualified to party's leadership. Ironically, the Muslim Brotherhood declared in 2007 that they may never allow women or Coptic Christians in decision-making positions, because this is contradictory to Islamic Sharia.[128] Yet, after the revolution, they did not hesitate to exploit women to polish the group's image and satisfy their political ambitions. In 2005 parliamentary elections, the Muslim Brotherhood listed only three women among the 133 candidates on their parliamentary election campaign platform. These women were the wives of prominent members in the group. They were politically weak and generally unpopular. One of them was

Makarem Eldiary, who included many items in her electoral program that were clearly discriminatory towards women.[129] Her equivalent in the post-revolution parliament was Azza Al-Garf who had been lobbying against the 2003 legislation that criminalized the savage practice of female genital mutilation.[130] A few weeks after her statements in support of female genital mutilation, the Muslim Brotherhood's "Freedom and Justice Party" launched a so-called "medical convoy" that roamed Upper Egyptian cities, where most population is poor and uneducated, searching for little girls to circumcise.[131]

The Spark of a Second Revolution:

The victory of Islamists in presidential and parliamentary elections, in 2012, was a result of disgraceful manipulation of people's religious piety and starvation for democratic change. The slogan the Salafists used in parliamentary elections, for example, was: "we are your way to Heaven."[132] They deceived the religious piteous grassroots citizens into believing that voting to Salafists is voting to Allah. However, within only a few months of Islamists' disappointing performance in parliament and presidency, the grassroots Egyptians realized the huge mistake they committed and became determined to fix it. Within only one year, Egyptians lost their patience over Muslim Brotherhood's discriminative beliefs and actions against women and Coptic Christians, in addition to Morsi's resounding failure in running state affairs or improving the economy.[133]

A series of surveys ran by Ibn Khaldun Center for Democratic Studies, between July 2012 and June 2013, about the public citizens' rates of satisfaction with presidential performance marked sharp declines in Islamists' popularity and credibility among grassroots citizens.[134] In July 2012, only one month after Morsi was elected, the Ibn Khaldun Center survey showed that 40.3% of Egyptians were satisfied with the performance of the president. During this month, Morsi – a new president then – gave an endless list of flowery promises that included improving the economy and empowering women and religious minorities into decision-making positions, in an unexpected contradiction to his group's principles.[135] That is probably what made the people optimistic about the future of Egypt under his leadership. In November 2012, amid a series of nonviolent demonstrations outside the presidential palace, protesting government's failure, the citizens' satisfaction index dramatically declined to 8.5%. The reason for this severe decline could be explained by the violent involvement of the militias of the Muslim Brotherhood in beating and torturing the nonviolent protesters, after the police forces refused to use violence to oppress the protests.[136]

By June 2013, in coincidence with Morsi's first anniversary in power, the Egyptian people decided that the Muslim Brotherhood have wasted their opportunity and does not deserve to remain in power, any longer. The persistence of Egyptians to overthrow the Muslim Brotherhood from power was clearly expressed through a number of nonviolent tactics that built up to the momentum of nation-wide nonviolent protests that

The Curious Case of the Three-Legged Wolf

overthrew Morsi from power, on his first anniversary as president, on the 30th of June, 2013.

Towards the end of 2012, ordinary citizens, especially in Cairo, started to hang banners outside their houses and shopping stores located on main streets, portraying Islamists as Machiavellian manipulators.[137] Soon after, a massive petition signing campaign, under the name "Tamarud" (i.e. Rebel), was launched by young liberal democratic activists to mobilize the "Couch Party" citizens to express their rejection to the Muslim Brotherhood regime. Tamarud petition collected more than twenty-two million signatures in less than three months, between February and June 2013, exceeding the number of those who voted to Morsi in the presidential elections.[138] Tamarud petition called upon Morsi to resign and for the constitutional court to set a date for new presidential elections.[139]

In parallel, young liberal activists organized protests, on regular Fridays, outside the Muslim Brotherhood's headquarters in Mokattam and outside the

President's Office in Heliopolis. As the police forces and military guards at the presidential office refused to use violence to control the nonviolent protesters, the Muslim Brotherhood's leaders ordered their militia youth to get involved.[140] The Muslim Brotherhood militia practiced extreme violence against protesters, who were highly committed to nonviolent discipline.[141]

The rising anger against the Muslim Brotherhood coupled with the military and police forces' decline to violently repress the nonviolent protesters, awakened people's nostalgia to living safely and quietly under a military regime. By March 2013, the protests against the Muslim Brotherhood started to incorporate slogans calling for military's return to political leadership. In addition to the regularly used slogan of "down with Muslim Brotherhood rule," the people started to chant the 2011 revolution's slogan "people and the military are one hand," once again. In April 2013, Ibn Khaldun Center for Democratic Studies ran a public opinion poll that asked Egyptian citizens about the extent of their acceptance of the military returning to taking political leadership.[142] The surveyed sample included two thousand people from different political, social, and intellectual backgrounds with sixty-three per cent of them under the age of thirty-five years old. The sample included residents from both rural and urban cities, all over Egypt. Eighty-two per cent agreed that "the military should return in power as soon as possible to reinstate security and stability."

This renewed confidence in military, encouraged the Minister of Defense, Abdel Fattah Al-Sisi, who was hired by the Muslim Brotherhood in August 2012, to instruct the military institution to take the side of the people against the Muslim Brotherhood.[143] That was not the first time, Al-Sisi takes the side of the people against an undesired political regime. He was the Director of Military Intelligence and a member of the Supreme Council of Armed Forces (SCAF) when the 2011 revolution erupted. Along with SCAF members, he participated in making the decision to abandon Mubarak and side with the young revolutionaries.

On the 1st of July, 2013, as the nonviolent protests calling for Morsi's resignation multiplied and expanded, Al-Sisi made a public statement, in his capacity as the Minister of Defense, giving Morsi an ultimatum of forty-eight hours to resign and organize early presidential elections, in compliance with people's demands. Few hours later, major state institutions – e.g. the police forces, the Central Church, Al-Azhar, and the judiciary – echoed the Minister of Defense's statement. On the next day, the 2nd of July, Morsi responded by convening a televised conference, wherein he made a long redundant speech about his electoral legitimacy and his determination to keep it, even if this required shedding blood.[144] His statements were publically understood as incitement to Muslim Brotherhood militia and religious piteous supporters to wage jihad against the nonviolent protesters. Indeed, a few minutes after the speech, violent clashes between Muslim Brotherhood's militia and anti-Morsi protesters erupted at several locations across Egypt, resulting in fatalities.

The Curious Case of the Three-Legged Wolf

On the 3rd of July, Morsi broke the forty-eight hours ultimatum by insisting to remain in his office and refusing to resign, in compliance with people's demands and military's pressure. Therefore, the military leadership convened a meeting with representatives of Tamarud movement, Al-Azhar, the Central Church, the Salafist Al-Nour party, the Public Intelligence, the Police Forces, and some public figures. Then, a televised statement was made by Al-Sisi and the participants of the meeting, wherein they announced the removal of Morsi, in response to protester's demands, handing temporary power to the head of the constitutional court, and taking necessary measures to write a new constitution and convene new presidential elections.[145]

Muslim Brotherhood's Violent Response Backfired:

Rather than yielding to the will of the people, the Muslim Brotherhood launched a relentless violent war on civilians, policemen, and state institutions, all over Egypt. The first victims of Muslim Brotherhood violent attacks were

Coptic Christian citizens in Upper Egypt, whose personal properties and churches were burnt and destroyed by angry Islamist affiliates. In one day, the violent affiliates of the Muslim Brotherhood and sympathizing Salafists burnt and destroyed eighty-three churches and attacked a dozen of police stations.[146] One graphic example was the horrible attack on Kerdasa Police Station, in Giza, where Muslim Brotherhood affiliates tortured police officers, using Nitric Acid, and then burnt them alive.[147]

Simultaneously, Muslim Brotherhood leaders, who fled Egypt immediately after the 2013 revolution, deliberately incited and funded their associates in the terrorist organization of Hamas in Gaza to "spread terror in Sinai."[148] Sinai is a strategic city in Eastern Egypt on borders with Israel. Hamas, which declares itself as a branch of the Muslim Brotherhood in Palestine,[149] could easily access North Sinai through illegitimate tunnels, which the Egyptian military flooded and blocked later in 2015.[150] In immediate response to Muslim Brotherhood leaders' incitement, Hamas attacked military troops in Sinai, and consequently revived fellow terrorist organizations that had been hiding in Sinai for years – e.g. Ansar Beit Al-Maqdes and Al-Jama'a Al-Islamia.[151] The waves of terrorism that Hamas initiated, at that time, was polarized in mid-2016, when the terrorist organizations in Sinai got united under the flag of the Islamic State (ISIS) and called themselves "Welayat Sinai."[152]

The peak of violent attacks by Muslim Brotherhood members and sympathizers inside Egypt continued till late 2015, mounting up to more than three thousand documented violent atrocities committed by the Muslim Brotherhood members and sympathizers against innocent civilians and state institutions in internal cities.[153] This horrific number of documented violent atrocities does not include the toll of life losses caused by terrorists dwelled in Sinai. One heartbreaking example that sums up the horrific scene in Sinai, after Hamas terrorist intervention in 2013, is the terrorist attack committed by forty terrorists on Al-Rawda Mosque in Bier Al-Abd City in North Sinai, in November 2017. The terrorist attack led to the merciless murder of more than three hundred helpless men and children, while performing Friday prayers. That goes without mentioning the hundreds of young military officers and soldiers, who has been killed in direct confrontations with terrorist groups in Sinai, due to the scarcity of reliable statics and information on military's war and development activities in Sinai.

The Big Lie of the Peaceful Rabaa Camp:

As Muslim Brotherhood affiliates were practicing violence against civilians in avenge to their ouster from power, Muslim Brotherhood leaders with good connections in the United States and Europe cleverly sold a big lie to Western media in an attempt to legitimize their violent atrocities inside Egypt.

While the anti-Morsi protesters gathered in Tahrir Square to celebrate his ouster, on the 3rd of July, Muslim Brotherhood gathered a few hundreds of their members and sympathizers from the Salafist grassroots affiliates into two parallel sit-in camps in Al-Nahda Square

The Curious Case of the Three-Legged Wolf

in Giza and Rabaa Square in Cairo. The Muslim Brotherhood manipulated the strikers, mostly poor and uneducated, into believing that the Egyptian military is launching a war on Islam.[154] Then, Muslim Brotherhood leaders contacted Western media and international human rights organizations to sell them the lie that the sit-ins are nonviolent camps that rejected the so-called "military coup" against Morsi. In reality, the strike camps of the Muslim Brotherhood were hubs for organizing and launching violent attacks on civilians and state facilities, as was revealed later through independent judicial investigations and documented confessions by Muslim Brotherhood members.[155]

Even worse, the Muslim Brotherhood leaders ordered the torture of the group's young members, who denounced using the strikes to organize violent attacks against civilians. On July 23rd, a group of six hundred and seventy (670) young members of the Muslim Brotherhood announced their dissidence from the group and called themselves "Muslim Brothers against Violence."[156] In response, the Muslim Brotherhood leaders arrested them, kept them in custody at Rabaa sit-in camp, and slashed and tortured them as punishment for dissent.[157]

In addition, the Muslim Brotherhood leaders forced women and children to join the strikes, in an attempt to let a Syria-style scenario unfold in Egypt, so they can easily call for foreign intervention on humanitarian basis.[158] They forced women to join their husbands on the strike to provide them with sexual intimacy whenever they need, so that they guarantee the men would remain in the strikes for longer.[159] They, also, brought children, under ten years old, from orphan houses owned by the group's charity organizations in rural poor cities, and forced the kids to carry coffins and wear labels reading "potential martyrs" on their chests.[160] This particular move backfired on the Muslim Brotherhood, rather winning them sympathy, as a number of human rights organizations condemned the Muslim Brotherhood's abuse of children in the sit-ins and exposing them to the experience of death.[161]

The Curious Case of the Three-Legged Wolf

In August 2016, Muslim Brotherhood's fabrications about the "peacefulness" of Rabaa and Al-Nahda strike camps were revealed by Ahmed Al-Moghier, the manager of Rabaa strike camp. He posted on his own Facebook page the full details on how they used the camps to hide machine guns, create primitive bombs and Molotov bottles, and train strikers on martial combat. He, also, confessed that they brought some skillful gunmen from the Muslim Brotherhood militia, to kill the police officers employed by a legal order from the Public Prosecutor to evacuate the strikes.[162] Al-Moghier's confessions derives their credibility from the fact that he was not only the manager of Rabaa strike, but also a close associate to Khairat Al-Shatter, the most powerful man and the *de facto* leader of the Muslim Brotherhood.

During the strike, in August 2013, a number of local human rights non-governmental organizations formed a fact checking delegation to visit Rabaa strike camp, after citizens living around Rabaa Square filed complaints to the Public Prosecutor about strikers receiving martial combat training and storing weapons at wooden coffins, located inside the strike camp. Al-Moghier and his armed affiliates prevented the human rights delegation from entering the strike camp or searching the wooden coffins. When the members of the delegation insisted, Al-Moghier and his men physically assaulted them, forcing them to leave.[163]

The military leadership, with the help of the judiciary, Al-Azhar, and the Prime Minister, spent long weeks hopelessly trying to convince the Muslim Brotherhood leaders to end the sit-ins, before Eid Al-Fitr.[164] Some foreign allies, including representatives from the European Union, the United States, and some Arab countries tried to intervene, in vain, to negotiate a deal with the leaders of the Muslim Brotherhood.[165] As reports and complaints were filed to the Public Prosecutor about the violent crimes practiced by the strikers against civilian inhabitants around the sit-in locations, the Public Prosecutor made a decision that the strikes represent a threat to national security. Accordingly, the Public

The Curious Case of the Three-Legged Wolf

Prosecutor issued a legal order assigning police forces to intervene adequately to disperse the sit-in camps. The 13th of August was declared as an ultimatum for the Muslim Brotherhood to end the strikes before police intervention.

As the Muslim Brotherhood leaders failed to comply, the police forces were sent on the early morning of the 14th of August to disperse the camps. According to eye witnesses and judicial investigations, conducted later, the assigned police forces aimed at gradual use of force and vowed commitment to high levels of self-discipline, while accomplishing their mission.[166] The policemen started by clearing a safe exit passage for the strikers to leave peacefully, without being harmed or arrested. Then, a policeman spoke to strikers, through a microphone, urging them to leave the strike camp without resistance.[167] In less than half an hour, a gunshot coming from inside the strike camp in Rabaa killed the policeman holding the microphone.[168] As a result, the police forces had to use force to deal with the shooters located inside the camp. Inevitably, the evacuation of the Rabaa camp turned into a horrific scene of mutual war between police forces and gunmen inside the strike. According to official statistics, more than six hundred people were killed, including policemen and civilians.[169]

The Curious Case of the Three-Legged Wolf

Declaring the Muslim Brotherhood a Terrorist Organization:

As the vengeful violent atrocities committed by the Muslim Brotherhood continued to increase and expand, in December 2013; Egypt, the United Arab Emirates, and Saudi Arabia declared the Muslim Brotherhood a terrorist organization.[170] As a result, they banned all Muslim Brotherhood activities, froze their assets and businesses, and listed Muslim Brotherhood leaders, who fled to Qatar, Turkey, Germany, UK, and US, on Interpol's red list. Meanwhile, a number of American and Egyptian civil society groups, intensified their lobbying at the United States, asking for the US administration to officially designate the Muslim Brotherhood as an international terrorist organization.[171]

Nevertheless, the Muslim Brotherhood ascribed their group, for decades, as the primary political representative of Muslims in the West. Despite its limited size compared to the majority moderate Muslims living in Europe and the United States, the Muslim Brotherhood enjoyed a privileged access to policy-makers and media, thanks to the highly organized political structure of their group. The moderate Muslims in the West are ordinary citizens, who practice their religion within their families and tend to identify themselves within the secular identity of the Western countries they belong to. Kamal Elhelbawy, the first founder of the Muslim Brotherhood in UK, said in an interview in 2005: "there are not many members [of the Muslim Brotherhood] here [in UK], but many Muslims in Britain intellectually support the aims of the Muslim Brotherhood."[172] Yet, with the recent rise of the threat of Islamic extremism, resulted by the formation of Al-Qaeda and ISIS, the West started to pay closer attention to the activities of political Islamist organizations and Muslim-owned charities and civil society organizations, including those affiliated to the Muslim Brotherhood. Despite federal investigations,[173] court decisions,[174] and congressional hearings[175] proving Muslim Brotherhood's involvement in enabling and funding violent Jihadists in the Middle East, the Western countries hosting Muslim Brotherhood members and operations are still incapable of making the decision to designate the Muslim Brotherhood as a terrorist organization.

The United States:

In his electoral campaign, US President Donald Trump, promised to designate the Muslim Brotherhood as an international terrorist organization and accordingly ban their activities inside the United States.[176] As soon as Trump was seated as president, in 2017, the American civil society organizations affiliated to the Muslim Brotherhood spread media statements accusing him of "Islamophobia,"[177] while convening devious cultural dialogue programs in partnership with major American Jewish organizations,[178] to wash away their jihadist record and discredit Trump's call to hold the group accountable.

Meanwhile, they falsely claimed that the Muslim Brotherhood is not a monolithic organization; i.e. each Muslim Brotherhood affiliate can manifest differently. This devious and completely untrue argument implied that the group's affiliates in Europe or the United States are not responsible for the violent atrocities committed by their affiliates in the Middle East. As a result, it became too complicated of an issue for the US Administration to designate the group, as a one whole entity, as a terrorist organization.[179] Yet, there are some simple facts that refute this ill argument.

The terrorist group Hamas, as one example of many, was founded by the donation money collected by Brotherhood-affiliated organizations in the West, under the false title of charity.[180] While the Muslim Brotherhood affiliates were committing violent attacks in Egypt after their ouster from political power, in 2013, Erdogan's party in Turkey was leading an international campaign to provide them with political cover and justify their use of violence against civilians and state facilities.[181] This highly orchestrated work between Muslim Brotherhood's jihadist, political, religious and civil factions proves that the Muslim Brotherhood is a one whole monolithic group, which activities should be banned.

The Curious Case of the Three-Legged Wolf

Europe:

On the other hand, Europe's reaction to citizens' concerns over the Muslim Brotherhood was divided into three directions. Some European countries, like France for example, adopted a highly cautious policy by severely banning all practices that is related to Islam, including banning the Muslim woman's traditional hijab.[182] Some other European countries, Germany for instance, adopted a relatively moderate approach, by curbing the space allowed for Muslim Brotherhood to operate as an organization within certain boundaries.

In 2014, Germany's Federal Office for Protecting the Constitution (BfV) created a database of Muslim Brotherhood members and started to closely monitor their activities for detecting potential acts of extremism.[183] In June 2015, Ahmed Mansour, the prominent media presenter on Aljazeera Network and renowned member of the Muslim Brotherhood, was arrested while in

Berlin. The charges against him included conducting televised interviews with Islamic jihadists and inciting and practicing violence against civilians in Egypt during and after the 2011 revolution.[184]

Some other European countries, such as Turkey and the United Kingdom, showed much tolerance towards the Muslim Brotherhood, despite the evident threat they represent on the national security of their countries and the world. It is fairly understood that Erdogan's regime is friendly to the Muslim Brotherhood. Erdogan is a member of the Muslim Brotherhood and his political party (AKP) is the Muslim Brotherhood's political organization in Turkey. Yet, it is confusing why Britain is still providing the Muslim Brotherhood with a safe haven to live and operate on its lands, despite the investigations that had proven the high level of threat that the Muslim Brotherhood imposes on the national security of Britain.[185]

The United Kingdom:

In April 2014, former Prime Minister David Cameron made the brave decision to officially investigate

The Curious Case of the Three-Legged Wolf

into the activities of the Muslim Brotherhood organization in the UK.[186] The purpose of the investigations was to decide whether the Muslim Brotherhood represented a risk to Britain's national security, given the fact that most Muslim Brotherhood leaders in the United Kingdom live and work with absolute freedom under the privileges of their British citizenship. British Intelligence bureaus – MI6 and MI5 – found this bold step, by Cameron, as a threat to their historical relationships with the Muslims Brotherhood. They described the investigations as "useless" and tried to convince Cameron to abort them.[187] The British intelligence depended on the Muslim Brotherhood, for decades, in controlling potential violent extremism among British Muslims, due to the vast expansion of Muslim Brotherhood's charity organizations, mosques, and schools all over Britain. Under the same ill logic, leading members of the British Parliament approached Cameron, personally, to convince him to abort the investigations. Allegedly, many British Members of Parliament, especially from the Labour Party, are having doubtful relationships with the Muslim Brotherhood.[188] The group's religious and charity dominance over nearly three million British Muslims makes them the perfect ally to politicians seeking to win such a huge bloc of Muslim voters.

Despite the pressure, Cameron ordered Sir John Jenkins, the first British state official to raise awareness about Muslim Brotherhood's linkage to violent extremism, to form a commission to lead the investigations. The members of the commission, which was formed in early April 2014, included: Sir John Jenkins as its head; Sir Kim Darroch, the Prime Minister's National Security Adviser; Sir John Sawers, Chief of the Secret Intelligence Service (MI6); and Charles Farr, Director General of the Office for Security and Counter Terrorism in the Home Office, who participated with Sir Jenkins on writing the final review report. Sir Jenkins' Commission's review relied on different resources of unswerving information from Britain and the Middle East, especially Egypt where the Muslim Brotherhood organization was founded a century ago. Sir

The Curious Case of the Three-Legged Wolf

Jenkins' Commission concluded its work on November 2014, yet nothing from the review was published till December 2015.

On 17th of December 2015, the Parliament released only a brief report on review findings to the public. There was, allegedly, a great pressure on Sir Jenkins' Commission not to publish the final review of investigations, because of its clear condemnation to the Muslim Brotherhood as a "violent jihadist" organization. The findings report of Sir Jenkins' Commission stated that "the Muslim Brotherhood is guilty of practicing, funding, and inciting violent extremism and embracing it as a core ideology." The findings report described the group as a "violent extremist organization that poses a danger to British safety and values of secularism."[189] Rather than celebrating Sir Jenkins' Commission findings, British media stations, either biased to or owned by the Muslim Brotherhood, claimed that Arab Gulf countries played a hand in the review.[190] Meanwhile, MI6 and MI5 held meetings with Muslim Brotherhood leaders to assure them that the investigation's findings report should not affect their ongoing relationship and cooperation.

As Cameron left the Prime Minister's office in July 2016, the Muslim Brotherhood caught their breath back. Theresa May, the new Prime Minister and a leading member at the Conservative Party, extended a friendly hand to the Muslim Brotherhood, as soon as she came to power. In her first month in power, she welcomed Muslim Brotherhood members, fleeing from the Middle East, to seeking political asylum in Britain.[191] Four months later, in November 2016, the House of Common's Foreign Affairs Committee announced that it ran a new investigation into Muslim Brotherhood's linkage to violent extremism, and then published a full review acquitting the Muslim Brotherhood from the findings that Sir Jenkins' Commission reached.[192] The Foreign Affairs Committee review, hardly, depended on redundant commentaries from a handful of academicians studying Islamism and some members of the Muslim Brotherhood, including Ibrahim Mounir, the current

The Curious Case of the Three-Legged Wolf

Deputy Guide of the organization, and the grandson of Hasan Al-Banna, Tariq Ramadan, who, in 2017, was found guilty of committing a series of sexual harassment and rape incidents to his female students.[193] The reviewers denied all Sir Jenkins' Commission evidence and confirmed that the group is political but not violent. The report of the Foreign Affairs Committee's review did not only acquit the Muslim Brotherhood from previously proven evidence on their involvement in practicing, inciting, and funding violent extremism, but also described the Muslim Brotherhood organization in the United Kingdom as a "firewall against violent extremism."[194]

Conclusion:
Lessons and Recommendations

Egypt's revolution and post revolution developments represent a curious case, which this research proved to be worthy of in-depth academic study and political comprehension, separated from the complicated context of the Arab Spring. The following are quick notes on the top lessons learnt throughout the long process of producing this dissertation, over five years of broad and intense academic investigations, and the researcher's decade of first-hand experience and direct involvement into the socio-political proceedings that took place before, during, and after the 2011 revolution and ultimately contributed to shaping Egypt's current reality.

The Curious Case of the Three-Legged Wolf

(1)

Indeed, nonviolent action is the force more powerful. *Reverse nonviolent action* is as equally powerful, though. Since Gene Sharp's early research on the science behind nonviolent activism, the majority of academic research has been focusing on the dynamics and outcomes of the nonviolent strategies adopted by political activists against their powerful opponents, who are mostly violent. The change in opponent's behavior, over the course of the nonviolent conflict, from using violent repression to abstaining from using violence, is usually measured as a "response" forced by the nonviolent discipline of the dissent movement. However, Egypt's 2011 revolution and its aftermath introduced a whole new dynamic of nonviolent conflict that requires changing the way scholars analyze opponent's patterns of behavior towards the nonviolent movement.

As extensively explained in this research, the Egyptian military forces made a deliberate strategic decision to use "reverse" nonviolent tactics to accommodate dissent and affect the eventual outcomes of the revolution. Egyptian revolutionaries' remarkable commitment to nonviolent discipline was a determining factor in their success in ousting Mubarak's regime from power. Equally, military's adept employment of *reverse nonviolent strategies* and high commitment to nonviolent discipline, which went far beyond negative cooperation with dissent by declining to violently repress them, played a tremendous role in controlling the immediate outcomes of the revolution and military's eventual success in re-dominating political power.

Reverse nonviolent action is introduced as a new academic term, in this study. Yet, further research work is still needed to better understand the viability of reverse nonviolent action in managing political dissent, through discovering and analyzing more cases with similar conflict dynamics to Egypt's revolution. In most historical cases of popular uprisings, nonviolent action won against violent repression. But, whether traditional nonviolent tactics can be as equally effective in combating *"reverse nonviolent action"* remains an open question.

(2)

Bringing down a dictator should not be the end goal for the dissent's nonviolent movement. The building of an alternative feasible system of governance should be the ultimate goal of political dissent. Overthrowing a dictator is only one step in the advanced strategy of building the political future that the nonviolent movement seeks. Otherwise, the dissent movement will end up being marginalized and ignored.

In Egypt's Arab Spring scenario, the liberal democratic activists initiated the revolution with a dream to turn Egypt into a liberal democratic state. Regrettably, they had no clear vision on how to fill in the vacuum in political power after the fall of Mubarak. As a result, the liberal democratic movement and its idealist goals ended up being marginalized and then thwarted, while the state turned from a corrupt autocracy under Mubarak into a manipulative theocracy ruled by political Islamists from the Muslim Brotherhood in presidency and the Salafist movement in parliament. Two years later, the liberal democratic activists had to replay their efforts in mobilizing grassroots citizens through a petition-signing campaign, and then leading a second popular upheaval that successfully ejected the Muslim Brotherhood's regime in mid-2013. Yet, once again, the liberal democratic movement was guilty of not having a clear vision on what should happen thereafter. As the violent vengeful reaction of the Muslim Brotherhood threatened the stability and security of the national state, the majority Egyptians passed political power to the military, in complete disregard to the role of the liberal democratic activists.

Therefore, the next steps after the fall of a dictator should be on the top priority list of the nonviolent movement, and should be publicly shared with and comprehensively appreciated by the grassroots supporters of the movement, from the very beginning.

(3)

Democracy is not a magic wand that can solve all flaws within state's economic and political structure. Building democracy is a process that may backfire on the usually idealist dissent movement and threaten the wellbeing of the national state, if not adequately implemented within a ripe context of social and political stability. In most historical cases of popular uprisings against dictator regimes, the grassroots citizens fall an easy prey to the momentum of mass voting on all and every state affair, during the aftermath of toppling the dictator. Usually, the illusionary democratic practice of voting is misunderstood as the magic door to a new era marked by more political freedom and less social and economic burdens. However, it does not take long for the citizens to bitterly discover that their votes have been abused to give legitimacy and power to the wrong politicians.

Egypt was not immune to such scenario. The intense practice of voting, under the illusion of building democracy after the fall of Mubarak, enabled Muslim Brotherhood's theocracy to replace Mubarak's autocracy. The Islamists played on grassroots citizens' religious piety to win political votes. The Egyptian grassroots citizens used to live under an extremely corrupt state of illiberal democracy under Mubarak, for three decades. They thought that Islamists won't be as corrupt or manipulative as Mubarak's regime. Thus, they gave the wrong vote to the wrong parties for the wrong reasons. The people were deceived by the illusion of democracy disguised in the immature practice of voting, which eventually led to failure and disappointment.

Nevertheless, if democracy is not the magic wand, liberal democracy should be the right path to follow and the most viable goal to seek. The grassroots citizens should not prioritize voting to some political party or group to fill in the power vacuum after the fall of the dictator. Rather, they should collectively focus on reaching an agreement on a feasible strategy to enable the ideals of liberal democracy as the ground base for the new state, regardless of who ends up dominating political power. Nonviolent movements, especially those preaching liberal democratization as an alternative system of governance, should target their grassroots supporters with educational programs on the values of liberal democracy as part of the movement's overall quest to bring down the dictator regime. Thus, the dissent movement will continue to keep devout and well-informed supporters till the end of the journey of not only bringing down a dictator, but most importantly building up a liberal democratic state.

(4)

Political polarization of the citizens is the most common trap that a country usually stumbles upon, after a nonviolent revolution that overthrows a hardliner dictator regime. Egypt is a living example on this argument. After the fall of Mubarak, people were divided into "revolutionaries" against "felol" (a term used, then, to describe Mubarak sympathizers and apologists). The "felol" accused the revolutionaries of being spies to some foreign government that wanted to destroy Egypt, while the revolutionaries accused the "felol" of being tolerant to corruption and less patriotic. While the "felol" and the revolutionaries got caught in endless battles over the legitimacy of their opposing political stances, the political Islamists sneaked their way up to parliament and presidency. Ironically, the revolutionaries and the "felol" joined forces, later in 2013, to wage a new nonviolent attack on Islamists and ejected them out of power. However, after the fall of the Muslim Brotherhood, the society got extremely polarized into two new political groups: anti-political-Islamism and Pro-political-Islamism. As religiously and politically complicated the concept of "political Islamism" is, the societal polarization was too extreme to the extent that it led to tragic cases of marital divorce and job firing.

The Curious Case of the Three-Legged Wolf

It is the responsibility of the nonviolent movement to prevent this polarization from happening, through accommodating and integrating the social groups affected by the fall of the dictator regime, rather than engaging into a useless wrestling over patriotic virtues and political merits. The goal of the nonviolent dissent movement should be to understand and accept the motives of their opposing groups and find ways to contain them, rather than challenging them into resenting the movement and its causes.

(5)

The politicization of civil society is an upsetting debacle that Egypt has fallen into, as a side effect to the political interactions leading up to the 2011 revolution. Due to the weakness of opposition political parties under Mubarak, the young political activists resorted to non-governmental human rights organizations to express their desire for change and practice political activism. While this strengthened the structure and effectiveness of civil society, it turned civil society organizations into a community of masked political parties. Towards the end of Mubarak's era, human rights organizations were publicly categorized under political labels such as: liberal groups, socialist/ Nasserist groups, and Islamist groups.

The Egyptian civil society played a tremendous role in introducing young political activists to the concept of nonviolent action and strategies, which was a determining factor in the success of the revolution against Mubarak, in 2011. However, after the fall of Mubarak, civil society organizations continued to play a political role that negatively affected their neutrality and undermined their credibility. This, indirectly, enabled furious media attacks on civil society organizations and professionals. Some local media outlets went as far as describing civil society organizations as paid agents to foreign intelligence bureaus.

The civil society professionals, especially those working for human rights organizations, in countries going through political transition after a nonviolent revolution, should be conscious of their political biases, at all times. They should not allow their individual political stances or preferences to intervene with their civil work for promoting and advancing civil and political rights. The civil society is one of the most important pillars of the liberal democratic state. Once the civil society loses its credibility over the political biases of its operatives, the formation of the aspired liberal democratic system of governance will become too complicated to realize.

(6)

Foreign intervention during a nonviolent conflict or a popular uprising is not always disadvantageous. Unlike what most scholars on nonviolent action advise, foreign support to the nonviolent dissent against a dictator is sometimes critical to the success of the uprising, as much as to, keeping the integrity of the national state after the removal of the dictator regime. In Egypt's case, the friendly intervention by US military generals, relying on their historical friendship with the leaders of the Egyptian military, played a significant role in defining the strategy the military adopted to handle the revolution and its consequences. On the other hand, foreign support to Egyptian civil society organizations, before the revolution, tremendously helped in disseminating knowledge about nonviolent action and strategies among the liberal democratic activists, who successfully used this knowledge later in toppling Mubarak's regime. Therefore, the question is not whether to encourage foreign meddling between political power and dissent, but when and how this meddling should be executed and who to implement it.

(7)

Political Islamism is a plague that the world needs to remedy, without fretting over the misleading concept of "Islamophobia." Eliminating political Islamism does not threaten Islam as a religion or the majority moderate Muslims, worldwide, in any way. Political Islamism is a cover to Islamic extremism, which embraces violent jihad against all signs of modern life, including secular systems of governance and national states. Egyptians learnt this lesson, the hard way, through facing thousands of vengeful violent atrocities committed by the Muslim Brotherhood, after the group's ouster from power, in mid-2013.

Violent jihad to spread Sharia Law overseas and replace western secular governments with Islamic Caliphate system is a core ideology that the Muslim Brotherhood dearly embraces. "Jihad is our way; dying in the way of Allah is our highest hope" is the motto of the Muslim Brotherhood. Their logo is a combination of two crossed swords and the word "prepare" which is taken from a Qur'anic verse instructing jihad against disbelievers of Islam. The Muslim Brotherhood is, evidently, the parent organization to all forms of Islamic terrorists threatening our world today. Osama Ben Laden, Al-Qaeda leader, his partner Abdullah Azzam, and Ayman Al-Zawahiry who took over Al-Qaeda after Ben Laden's death, were all members of the Muslim Brotherhood before they built their own terrorist organization.[195] Most of the young men, who fled Egypt to join the "Islamic State in Iraq and Sham - ISIS," after 2013, were active members of the Muslim Brotherhood, where they received their initial training on violent jihad.[196] Abu Bakr Al-Bughdady, the founding leader of ISIS started his life as a teen member of the Muslim Brotherhood.[197]

Most of the violent Islamic terrorists, threatening the security of our world today, act as "lone wolves." They are brainwashed youth, who attack their own families and neighbors, under the illusion of some jihad inciting fatwas, similar to those instated by Yusif Al-Qaradawi, the spiritual leader of the Muslim Brotherhood. Several studies proved that a lone wolf needs nothing more than an enabling environment, where sheikhs and religious mentors incite violent extremism against non-Muslims as a form of divine-approved jihad.[198] That is exactly what the Muslim

The Curious Case of the Three-Legged Wolf

Brotherhood is providing to violent extremists, who are threatening the security of our world, at the present time.

The lenient policy the United States, the United Kingdom, and Europe are currently adopting towards the Muslim Brotherhood, out of fear of being stigmatized as "Islamophobic," is expected to backfire on them, sooner or later. The Muslim Brotherhood's charity networks in the United States and Britain are not only abusing the open society in these countries as a hub to collect donation money and spend it on terrorists in the Middle East. Even worse, they are offering a supporting environment to radicalizing Western youth through their widely spread mosques, charities, and schools, which promote violent jihad as an honor every Muslim should pursue.

When you see a snake in your home, you do not cuddle it, but hit it on the head till it falls dead. If violent extremism is the snake, the Muslim Brotherhood is the head of the snake that the world should unite to fight to the end.

Dalia Ziada

The Curious Case of the Three-Legged Wolf

Endnotes and References

[1] Gene Sharp, "Social Power and Political Freedom" (Extending Horizons Books, Porter Sargent Publishers, Inc., 1980), p.26

[2] ibid, p.25

[3] ibid, p.27

[4] ibid, p. 219

[5] Peter Ackerman and Jack DuVall, "A Force More Powerful: A Century of Nonviolent Conflict" (St. Martin Press, New York, Hardcover 2000), p.7

[6] ibid, p.2

[7] Gene Sharp, "Social Power and Political Freedom" (Extending Horizons Books, Porter Sargent Publishers, Inc., 1980), p.24

[8] ibid, p.27

[9] ibid, p.57

[10] ibid, p.365

[11] ibid, p. 368

[12] ibid, p.195

The Curious Case of the Three-Legged Wolf

[13] Danielle Pletka and Ali Alfoneh, "Iran's Hidden Revolution" (The New York Times, June 16, 2009) -
Link: http://www.nytimes.com/2009/06/17/opinion/17pletka.html

[14] I was personally involved in helping the Iranian activists use proxy tools in order not to be tracked by security forces, especially on Twitter. Egyptian bloggers were extremely interested in the Iranian revolution as we believed that the success of the revolution in Iran would inspire a stronger revolution in Egypt.

[15] Data and statistics are collected from the United Nations' "World Population Prospects" database (United Nations, Department of Economic and Social Affairs, Population Division, 2010) -
Link: http://www.un.org/en/development/desa/publications/world-population-prospects-the-2010-revision.html

[16] See "Tunisia" chapter in the "International Religious Freedom Report 2010" (US Department of State, Bureau of Democracy, Human Rights, and Labor, July-December 2010) -
Link: https://www.state.gov/j/drl/rls/irf/2010_5/168277.htm

[17] See "Egypt" chapter in the "International Religious Freedom Report 2010" (US Department of State, Bureau of Democracy, Human Rights, and Labor, July-December 2010) -
Link: https://www.state.gov/j/drl/rls/irf/2010_5/168262.htm

[18] Ashraf Abdel Hamid, "Al-Tayeb answers questions on why Al-Azhar follows Al-Ashaari School" (Alarabiya TV wesbsite, April 25, 2015) -
Link (in Arabic): http://ara.tv/yfram

[19] There are no reliable official data on the size of the Baha'i population in Egypt, because of a 1960 Decree that annulled their status as a recognized group, and thus prevented them from registering the newborn as Baha'i at state official records. For more information on the status of the Baha'is of Egypt, see:
https://minorityrights.org/minorities/bahai-of-egypt/

[20] Alessandra Bajec, "The battle between secularism and Muslim identity in Tunisia during Ramadan" (The New Arab, In-Depth, June 8, 2018) –
Link: https://www.alaraby.co.uk/english/indepth/2018/6/8/secularism-and-muslim-identity-in-tunisia-during-ramadan

[21] Example: Rached Ghannouchi's the Islamic Tendency Movement, which turned later into Ennahda Islamic Movement, and then Ennahda Party after Tunisia's 2010 revolution.
See: Ramazan Yildirim, "Transformation of the Ennahda Movement from Islamic Jama'ah to Political Party" (in Insight Turkey Journal, SETA Foundation for Political, Economic and Social Research, Vol. 19, No. 2, Spring 2017), pp. 189-214.

[22] Suliman Shafik et al., "Egyptian Copts between Two Revolutions" (Dar Amaly for Publishing, Hardcover, in Arabic, 2014), pp.37-77.
[23] Gihan Shahine, "Risks to Al-Azhar?" (Focus, Al-Ahram Weekly, Issue 1157, July 18-24, 2013) –
Link: http://weekly.ahram.org.eg/News/3403.aspx

[24] Editor, "World's First Documented Labor Strike Took Place in Ancient Egypt In The 12th Century BC" (Ancient History Facts, Featured Stories, Ancient Pages, June 7, 2016) -
Link: http://www.ancientpages.com/2016/06/07/worlds-first-documented-labor-strike-took-place-in-ancient-egypt-in-the-12th-century-bc/

[25] Alan H. Gardiner, "The Eloquent Peasant" (in The Journal of Egyptian Archaeology, Vol. 9, No. 1/2, Sage Publications, Ltd., April 1923), pp. 5-25

[26] Gene Sharp, "Social Power and Political Freedom" (Extending Horizons Books, Porter Sargent Publishers, Inc., 1980), p.25

[27] Lawrence Wright, "The Looming Tower: Al-Qaeda and the Road to 9/11" (Alfred A. Knopf, Inc., 2006), p.29

[28] Example: Al-Maududi movement in Pakistan, for more in its relationship to the Muslim Brotherhood in Egypt, see: Lorenzo Vidino, "The New Muslim Brotherhood in the West", (Columbia University Press, 2010)

[29] Ahmed Al-Tayeb, "Tradition and Renewal: Discussions and Answers" (Dar Al-Quds Al-Araby for Publishing, 2nd Edition, 2016), p. 8.

[30] Said K. Aburish, "Nasser, the Last Arab" (St. Martin's Press, 2004), p. 141.

[31] Ahmed Al-Tayeb, "Tradition and Renewal: Discussions and Answers" (Dar Al-Quds Al-Araby for Publishing, 2nd Edition, 2016), pp. 9-10.

[32] Ibid, p. 12.

[33] Wahabis is an eighteenth-century Islamist movement, founded by Muhammad ibn Abd al-Wahhab, in Saudi Arabia, calling for socio-moral reconstruction of society, based on Islamic Sharia.

[34] Assaf Moghadam, "The Globalization of Martyrdom: Al Qaeda, Salafi Jihad, and the Diffusion of Suicide Attacks" (The Johns Hopkins University Press, 2008), pp. 99-103.

[35] William E. Farrell, "Five Sadat Assassins Executed in Egypt" (The New York Times, April 16, 1982) –
Link: https://www.nytimes.com/1982/04/16/world/5-sadat-assassins-executed-in-egypt.html

[36] Despite the peace treaty with Israel in 1979, the Egyptian state continues to celebrate the 6th of October, which marks the 1973 war against Israel in Sinai, as Egypt's National Day and the Armed Forces Anniversary.

[37] Aswan High Dam is an embankment dam built across the Nile in Aswan, south Egypt, in 1969, with the purpose to mitigate the effects of floods and use flood power in producing electricity. As a result, Egypt got greater political influence over the Nile River, which affected development goals of the nine African countries sharing the river with Egypt. See: Alastair Leithead, "The 'water war' brewing over the new River Nile dam" (in BBC Africa, February 24, 2018) – Link: https://www.bbc.com/news/world-africa-43170408

[38] Camp David Accord and the Peace Treaty are used alternatively in this research to refer to the peace agreement between Egypt and Israel, signed in March 1979.

[39] Fareed Zakaria, "The Future of Freedom: Illiberal Democracy at Home and Abroad" (W.W. Norton and Company, 2007), pp. 18-19.

[40] Ibid.

[41] Safia Al-Souhail et al., "Modern Narrative for Muslim Women in the Middle East: Forging a New Future" (The American Islamic Congress, 2010), p.14.

[42] Ibid.

[43] Michele Dunne and Amr Hamzawy, "Does Egypt Need International Election Observer?"(Carnegie Commentary, October 14th, 2010) – Link: http://carnegie-mec.org/publications/?fa=41733

[44] Bruce K. Rutherford, "Egypt after Mubarak: Liberalism, Islam, and Democracy in the Arab World" (Princeton University Press, 2008) p.1

[45] Fareed Zakaria, "The Future of Freedom: Illiberal Democracy at Home and Abroad" (W.W. Norton and Company, 2007), p. 142

[46] Tharwat Al-Kherbawy, "The Secret of the Temple: The Unrevealed Mysteries of the Muslim Brotherhood" (Dar Nahdet Misr Publishing Co., 2012), pp.131-133.

[47] Dalia Ziada, "It is not about Niqab, It's about Credibility" (Readers Room, Alt Muslimah, October 17, 2009) –
Link: http://www.altmuslimah.com/2009/10/its_not_about_niqab_its_about_credibility/

[48] Zainab Abdellah, "Al-Tayeb, Muslim Brotherhood's Foe" (Sout Al-Omma, June 30, 2018) –
Link: https://bit.ly/2CrpfEw

[49] Sarah El-Sirgany, "Muslim Brotherhood Students Dress as Militias in Al-Azhar Sit-in" (Daily News Egypt, December 12, 2006) –
Link: https://dailynewsegypt.com/2006/12/12/muslim-brotherhood-students-dress-as-militias-in-al-azhar-sit-in/

[50] Bradley Hope, "Khairat Al Shater – Muslim Brotherhood power broker and now target of Egyptian anger" (The National, July 2, 2013) –
Link: https://www.thenational.ae/world/mena/khairat-al-shater-muslim-brotherhood-power-broker-and-now-target-of-egyptian-anger-1.597207

[51] Madar Annahar, "Military Trials of the Muslim Brotherhood: Preliminary Attacks or Preparation for Presidential Hier" (Annahar Newspaper, Issue 240, in Arabic, May 2, 2008) –
PDF: http://www.annaharkw.com/ANNAHAR/Resources/PdfPages/02-05-2008/P37.pdf

[52] See the official web portal of "The World Organization of Al-Azhar Graduates" here: https://azhargraduates.org/en/

[53] The Grand Imam is the highest religious authority in the entire Muslim world, including Sunni and Shiite Muslims.

[54] See for example: Amr Al-Liethy, "Interview with the Grand Imam Ahmed Al-Tayeb on the Influence of Salafists on Al-Azhar", (Wahed Men Al-Nas, Dream TV, June 7, 2011) –
Video (in Arabic): https://www.youtube.com/watch?v=GUoCe7Uk7To

[55] Dawod Al-Shourian et al., "Interview with the New Grand Imam of Al-Azhar, Ahmed Al-Tayeb" (Wajeh Alsahafa, Al-Arabiya TV, in Arabic, April 3, 2010) –
Video (in Arabic): https://www.youtube.com/watch?v=r9uhzGyk9Eg

[56] Emad Eddin Hussien, "The Grand Imam: This is My Story with the Muslim Brotherhood" (Al-Shorouk Newspaper, in Arabic, January 1, 2015) –
Link (archived): http://bit.ly/2FJZVgl

[57] Shaaban Hadya, "The Muslim Brotherhood are Displeased by the Appointment of Ahmed Al-Tayeb as the Grand Imam of Al-Azhar" (Youm7 Newspaper, in Arabic, March 19, 2010) –
Link: http://www.youm7.com/203155

[58] "Al-Azhar and The Revolution: Documentary Analysis on Al-Azhar's Political Stances During and After Egypt's 2011 Revolution" (Al-Arabiya Institute for Arab Studies, October 15, 2012) –
Link: https://bit.ly/2AW42Tp

[59] Emad Eddin Hussien, "The Grand Imam: This is My Story with the Muslim Brotherhood" (Al-Shorouk Newspaper, in Arabic, January 1, 2015) –
Link (archived): http://bit.ly/2FJZVgl

[60] Article 4 of the Egyptian Constitution written in 2012, and Article 7 of the Egyptian Constitution, in effect since 2014, stipulate that: "Al-Azhar is an independent scientific Islamic institution, with exclusive competence over its own affairs. It is the main authority for religious sciences, and Islamic affairs. It is responsible for preaching Islam and disseminating the religious sciences and the Arabic language in Egypt and the world. The state shall provide enough financial allocations to achieve its purposes. Al-Azhar's Grand Imam is independent and cannot be dismissed. The method of appointing the Grand Imam from among the members of the Council of Senior Scholars is to be determined by law." –

See English Version of the Egyptian Constitution of 2012 here:
https://www.wipo.int/edocs/lexdocs/laws/en/eg/eg047en.pdf
See English version of the Egyptian Constitution of 2014 here:
https://www.constituteproject.org/constitution/Egypt_2014.pdf

[61] Safia Al-Souhail et al., "Modern Narrative for Muslim Women in the Middle East: Forging a New Future" (The American Islamic Congress, 2010), p.10.

[62] Daniela Pioppi, "The Judiciary and Revolution in Egypt" (Insight Egypt Journal, N.2, Istituto Affari Internazionali, August 2013) – PDF: http://www.iai.it/sites/default/files/inegypt_02.pdf

[63] Tina Rosenberg, "Revolution U: What Egypt Learned from the Students Who Overthrew Milosevic" (Foreign Policy Magazine, February 16, 2011) –
Link: http://www.foreignpolicy.com/articles/2011/02/16/revolution_u

[64] Sheryl Gay Stolberg, "Shy US Intellectual Created Playbook Used in a Revolution" (The New York Times, February 16th, 2011) –
Link: http://www.nytimes.com/2011/02/17/world/middleeast/17sharp.html?pagewanted=all

[65] See for example:
- Noah Mendel, "Can a Comic Book About MLK Change the Middle East (At Least a Little)?" (History News Network, May 10, 2009) –
  Link: http://www.hnn.us/articles/80834.html
- Ethan Vesely-Flad, "The Untold Story of How a FOR Comic Book Inspired Egyptian Revolutionaries" (Fellowship of Reconciliation, February 2, 2011) –

Link: http://forusa.org/blogs/ethan-vesely-flad/martin-luther-king-egypt-fellowship-reconciliation/8479
- Michael Cavna, "Amid Revolution, Arab Cartoonists Draw Attention to their Cause" (The Washington Post, March 7, 2011) –
Link: http://voices.washingtonpost.com/comic-riffs/2011/03/arab_cartoons.html

[66] The government used to justify the brutality of the police and the extension of the emergency of state by falsely claiming that they are only targeting terrorists, criminals, and thugs. But ordinary citizens would not be touched.

[67] News Editor, "Egypt Election: Hosni Mubarak's NDP Sweeps Second Round" (BBC Website, December 7, 2010) –
Link: http://www.bbc.co.uk/news/world-middle-east-11935368

[68] Michele Dunne and Amr Hamzawy, "From Too Much Egyptian Opposition to Too Little, and Legal Worries Besides" (Carnegie Endowment for International Peace, December 13, 2010) –
Link: http://carnegieendowment.org/2010/12/13/from-too-much-egyptian-opposition-to-too-little-and-legal-worries-besides/2ynu

[69] Michele Dunne and Amr Hamzawy, "Egypt's Unobserved Elections" (Carnegie Endowment for International Peace, November 23, 2010) –
Link: http://carnegieendowment.org/2010/11/23/egypt-s-unobserved-elections/35ke

[70] Lara Logan, "The Deadly Beating that Sparked Egypt Revolution" (CBS News, February 3, 2011) –
Link: http://www.cbsnews.com/2100-18563_162-7311469.html

[71] Gene Sharp, "Waging Nonviolent Struggle: 20th Century Practice and 21st Century Potential" (Extending Horizons Books, Porter Sargent Publishers, Inc., 2005), pp. 49-67

The Curious Case of the Three-Legged Wolf

[72] News Editor, "Egypt Army to Tackle Bread Crisis" (BBC Website, March 17, 2008) –
Link: http://news.bbc.co.uk/2/hi/middle_east/7300899.stm

[73] The Editor, "Egypt's State of Emergency Ends After 31 Years" (The Telegraph, May 31, 2012) –
Link: http://www.telegraph.co.uk/news/worldnews/africaandindianocean/egypt/9303195/Egypts-state-of-emergency-ends-after-31-years.html

[74] Luke Hardin, "US Reported Routine Police Brutality in Egypt, WikiLeaks Cables Show" (The Guardian, January 28, 2011) – Link: http://www.guardian.co.uk/world/2011/jan/28/egypt-police-brutality-torture-wikileaks

[75] Lara Logan, "The Deadly Beating that Sparked Egypt Revolution" (CBS News, February 3rd, 2011) – Link: http://www.cbsnews.com/2100-18563_162-7311469.html

[76] George Lakey, "The Sociological Mechanisms of Nonviolent Struggle" (Peace Research Reviews, Vol. II, no. 6, December 1968), p. 12.

[77] Gene Sharp, "Waging Nonviolent Struggle: 20th Century Practice and 21st Century Potential" (Extending Horizons Books, Porter Sargent Publishers, Inc., 2005), pp. 416-417.

[78] ibid, pp. 418-419.

[79] Interview with Mai Ibrahim, one of the protesters who was at Tahrir Square on the night of January 28, exclusive for the purpose of writing this paper.

[80] Sandro Contenta, "Protesters Stand Their Ground as Tanks Roll into Tahrir Square" (The Star, January 30, 2011) –
Link: http://www.thestar.com/news/world/article/930658--protesters-stand-their-ground-as-tanks-roll-into-tahrir-square

[81] Ben Wedeman, "Protesters Swarm Egyptian Army Vehicle" (CNN, January 28, 2011) -
Video:
http://cnn.com/video/?/video/world/2011/01/28/egypt.cairo.tank.protesters.cnn

[82] See this video for Nasser documenting the free officers plot of launching the 1952 revolution:
https://www.youtube.com/watch?v=wdd6E88BBQA

[83] See this archive documenting the Twitter Feed of Lieutenant Mohamed Wadi'e, one of the leaders of April 8th Movement – Link: https://bit.ly/2RAxqJb

[84] Gene Sharp, "Waging Nonviolent Struggle: 20th Century Practice and 21st Century Potential" (Extending Horizons Books, Porter Sargent Publishers, Inc., 2005), p. 417.

[85] ibid, p. 418.

[86] The Prisoner's dilemma can be generated within a regime through nonviolent strategy. Sustained and intense methods of nonviolent intervention and protest can limit communication between factions within a regime. Poor communication may lead to growing mistrust within the regime and an inability of regime factions to rely on each other and coordinate their responses.

[87] Peter Beaumont and Jack Shenker, "Egypt's Revolution Turns Ugly as Mubarak Fights Back" (The Guardian, February 2, 2011) –
Link: https://www.theguardian.com/world/2011/feb/02/egypt-revolution-turns-ugly

[88] Nick Fagge, "Camel Charge in the Battle for Cairo" (The Telegraph, February 4, 2011) –
Link: http://www.dailytelegraph.com.au/news/camel-charge-in-the-battle-for-cairo/story-e6freuy9-1225999796755

[89] Ahmed Youssif and Nevin Mosa'ad, "The Arab Nation 2011 – 2012: Complexities and Horizons of Change" (Center for Arab Unity Studies, May 2012), p.128 (in Arabic).

[90] Mohamed Saad Khattab, "Backstory of Mubarak's Last Hours in Office: The President Attempted to Remove Tantawy, So SCAF Decided to Abandon Mubarak" (Sout Al-Oma Newspaper, The Printed Version, July 24, 2011 - in Arabic).

[91] Ben Wedeman, "Egyptian History: Suleiman Announces Mubarak's Resignation and Crowd Reacts on Split Screen" (CNN, February 11, 2011) –
Video: http://youtu.be/lu0MxwX1Yr8

[92] Jeremy Sharp, "Egypt: Transition Under Military Rule" (Congressional Research Service, RL33003, June 21, 2012) –
PDF: https://www.everycrsreport.com/files/20120621_RL33003_fbec57cc2e470cca3db5c8319660f3ed0a98bd32.pdf

[93] This quote is taken from an interview conducted by the researcher with the US Joint Staff Spokesperson, in January 2012 for the exclusive purpose of producing this paper.

[94] ibid.

[95] ibid.

[96] ibid.

[97] Derek Lutterbeck, "Arab Uprisings and Armed Forces: Between Openness and Resistance" (The Geneva Center for the Democratic Control of Armed Forces, SSR Paper 2, 2011) –
PDF: https://www.dcaf.ch/sites/default/files/publications/documents/SSR_PAPER2.pdf

[98] Fareed Zakaria, "The Future of Freedom: Illiberal Democracy at Home and Abroad" (W.W. Norton and Company, 2007), p. 119.

[99] Lorenzo Vidino, "The New Muslim Brotherhood in the West", (Columbia University Press, 2010), pp. 208 - 212.

[100] Shaaban Hadya, "Muslim Brotherhood: We Don't Seek Presidency or Parliamentary Majority" (Youm7 Newspaper, March 23, 2011) – Link: http://www.youm7.com/375735

[101] Lorenzo Vidino, "Lessons Learnt: Post-Mubarak developments within the Egyptian Muslim Brotherhood" (Arts and Humanities Research Council, Public Policy Series, No.2, December 2011) – PDF: https://ahrc.ukri.org/documents/project-reports-and-reviews/ahrc-public-policy-series/post-mubarak-developments-within-the-egyptian-muslim-brotherhood/

[102] Nick Fagge, "Camel Charge in the Battle for Cairo" (The Telegraph, February 4, 2011) – Link: http://www.dailytelegraph.com.au/news/camel-charge-in-the-battle-for-cairo/story-e6freuy9-1225999796755

[103] Press Editor, "Inside Egypt: Poll Led by David Pollock Reveals Egyptian Public Views on Protests" (The Washington Institute for Near East Policy, February 9, 2011) – Link: https://www.washingtoninstitute.org/press-room/view/inside-egypt-poll-led-by-david-pollock-reveals-egyptian-public-views-on-pro

[104] Christopher Dickey, "The Real Reasons Saudi Crown Prince Mohammed bin Salman Wanted Khashoggi Dead or Alive" (The Daily Beast, October 21, 2018) – Link: https://www.thedailybeast.com/the-real-reasons-saudi-crown-prince-mohammed-bin-salman-wanted-khashoggi-dead

[105] Yusuf Al-Qaradawi is the Muslim Brotherhood's highest spiritual authority. He lived in and worked from Britain for decades, after fleeing Egypt in 1960s. But, in 2008 he was banned from entering Britain on the background of issuing fatwas that incite young Muslims in the West on practicing violent jihad. See for example: Vikram

Dodd, "Controversial Muslim cleric banned from Britain" (The Guardian, February 7, 2008) –
Link: https://www.theguardian.com/uk/2008/feb/07/religion.politics

[106] See this archive documenting the Twitter Feed of Lieutenant Mohamed Wadi'e, one of the leaders of April 8th Movement –
Link: https://bit.ly/2RAxqJb

[107] Ahmed Al-Behiery, "Thousands of Imams and Preachers Protest outside Al-Azhar Sheikhdom, Calling for the Resignation of the Grand Imam" (Almasry Alyoum, April 26, 2011) –
Link (in Arabic): https://www.almasryalyoum.com/news/details/127911

[108] News Editor, "Al-Tayeb's Adviser Denies the Grand Imam's Resignation" (Middle East News Agency, March 7, 2011) –
Link (in Arabic): http://www.youm7.com/365060

[109] Ahmed Al-Behiery, "Confrontations between Al-Tayeb and Qotub about the Protests Calling for Al-Azhar's Independence" (Almasry Alyoum, April 28, 2011) –
Link (in Arabic): https://www.almasryalyoum.com/news/details/128484

[110] Gihan Shahine, "Risks to Al-Azhar?" (Focus, Al-Ahram Weekly, Issue 1157, July 18-24, 2013) –
Link: http://weekly.ahram.org.eg/News/3403.aspx

[111] "Al-Azhar and The Revolution: Documentary Analysis on Al-Azhar's Political Stances During and After Egypt's 2011 Revolution" (Al-Arabiya Institute for Arab Studies, October 15, 2012) –
Link: https://bit.ly/2AW42Tp

[112] See the full text of Decree 13/2012 here (in Arabic):
http://www.laweg.net/Default.aspx?action=ViewActivePages&ItemID=75214&Type=6

[113] See Article 4 in the English Version of the Egyptian Constitution of 2012 here:
https://www.wipo.int/edocs/lexdocs/laws/en/eg/eg047en.pdf

[114] David Kirkpatrick, "Named Egypt's Winner, Islamist Makes History" (The New York Times, June 24, 2012) –
Link: https://www.nytimes.com/2012/06/25/world/middleeast/mohamed-morsi-of-muslim-brotherhood-declared-as-egypts-president.html

[115] Dalia Ziada, "Can Egypt Turn into Islamic State after Mubarak?" (Blogpost, February 10, 2011) –
Link: http://daliaziada.blogspot.com/2011/02/can-egypt-turn-into-islamic-state-after.html

[116] Eric Trager et al., "The Rise and Fall of Egypt's Muslim Brotherhood" (The Washington Institute for Near East Policy, Book Discussion, November 8, 2016) –
Link: https://www.washingtoninstitute.org/policy-analysis/view/the-rise-and-fall-of-egypts-muslim-brotherhood

[117] Tarek Sabry et al., "Investigations into Manipulating Presidential Elections 2012" (Elwatan Newspaper, January 21, 2016) - Link (in Arabic): https://www.elwatannews.com/news/details/928900

[118] World Youth Forum, "Open Discussion with President Elsisi on Libya, Syria, and Iraq" (Elwatan Newspaper, November 6, 2018) –
Link (in Arabic): https://www.elwatannews.com/news/details/3778296

[119] Dalia Ziada, "Egypt's Islamists: Much to Prove on Women's Rights" (CNN, June 28, 2012) –
Link: https://edition.cnn.com/2012/06/28/opinion/egypt-womens-rights/index.html

[120] Alaa Al-Din Arafat, "The Rise of Islamism in Egypt" (Springer International AG, 2017), p. 19

[121] Ernesto Londoño, "Egypt's Morsi replaces military chiefs in bid to consolidate power" (The Washington Post, August 12, 2012) –
Link: https://wapo.st/2CBhADl

[122] Maha Ben Abdel Azim, "Women's Rights in Egypt between the Fallen Regime and the Islamists" (France 24 Website, June 8, 2012) –
Link (in Arabic): https://bit.ly/2U068Zr

The Curious Case of the Three-Legged Wolf

[123] Mahmoud Alhadary, "Salafists' Historical Hatred towards the Egyptian Flag" (Mobtada News Agency, September 17, 2017) – Link (in Arabic): https://www.mobtada.com/details/651755

[124] Mahmoud Mosalam, "A Salafist Member of Parliament Recites Azan in Parliament, Disturbing Discussions" (Misr Toqarir, Alhayah TV, February 7th, 2012) – Video (in Arabic): https://www.youtube.com/watch?v=MVJ7hQk7NU4

[125] Dalia Ziada, "Egypt's Islamists: Much to Prove on Women's Rights" (CNN, June 28, 2012) – Link: https://edition.cnn.com/2012/06/28/opinion/egypt-womens-rights/index.html

[126] Safia Al-Souhail et al., "Modern Narrative for Muslim Women in the Middle East: Forging a New Future" (The American Islamic Congress, 2010), p.12.

[127] ibid, p. 14

[128] Tarek Salah and Mohamed Suliman, "The Muslim Brotherhood: We Hold Our Position against Empowering Women or Coptic Christians into Decision-making Positions" (Almasry Alyoum, March 14, 2011) – Link (in Arabic): https://www.almasryalyoum.com/news/details/119032

[129] Doaa Imam, "Makarem Al-Diery: The God-Mother of the Muslim Brotherhood who Fought against Women's Rights" (Almarjie Publication on Political Islamism, Profile, July 24, 2018) – Link (in Arabic): http://www.almarjie-paris.com/2726

[130] Sarah Darwish, "Female Members of Parliament Who Abandoned Women's Rights" (Youm7 Newspaper, October 18, 2015) – Link (in Arabic): http://www.youm7.com/2395640

[131] Dandrawy Elhawary, "Muslim Brotherhood's Convoy Circumcises Girls in Minya" (Youm7 Newspaper, May 13, 2012) – Link (in Arabic): http://www.youm7.com/676940

[132] Mohamed Elbahrawy and Mahmoud Othman, "Various Reactions over the Use of Religious Slogans in Electoral Campaigns" (Youm7 Newspaper, October 19, 2011) –
Link (in Arabic): http://www.youm7.com/515942

[133] Ashraf El-Sherif, "The Egyptian Muslim Brotherhood's Failures" (Carnegie Endowment for International Peace, Paper, July 1, 2014) –
Link: https://carnegieendowment.org/2014/07/01/egyptian-muslim-brotherhood-s-failures-pub-56046

[134] Mahmoud Hassouna, "Public Opinion Survey by Ibn Khaldun Center Reveals: 67% of Egyptians are not Satisfied with Morsi's Performance and Wants Him to Leave Power" (Elwatan Newspaper, November 22, 2012) –
Link (in Arabic): https://www.elwatannews.com/news/details/81386

[135] Ayat Alhabal and Amir Khaled, "Promises of Morsi for his First 100 Days in Power" (Elwatan Newspaper, June 25, 2012) –
Link (in Arabic): https://www.elwatannews.com/news/details/20666

[136] News Report, "Muslim Brotherhood Militia Attack Protesters at a Sit-in outside Al-Etihadiya" (Russia Today Arabic, December 5, 2012) –
Video (in Arabic): https://www.youtube.com/watch?v=91DUPoojKlo

[137] Dalia Ziada, "Why Political Islamist Should Eventually Fail in Political Power" (Blogpost, May 9, 2012) –
Link (in Arabic): http://daliaziada.blogspot.com/2012/05/blog-post.html

[138] News Report, "Tamarud Movement Announces Collecting 22 Million Signatures" (Sky News Arabia, June 29, 2013) –
Video (in Arabic): https://www.youtube.com/watch?v=dtXiePGuy_s

[139] Tamarud is a petition signing campaign that played a tremendous role in mobilizing grassroots Egyptians to rebel against the Muslim Brotherhood regime in June 2013 – See, for example, BBC's profile on Tamarud here: https://www.bbc.com/news/world-middle-east-23131953

The Curious Case of the Three-Legged Wolf

[140] News Editor, "The Presidential Military Guard Refuses to Use Violence against Protesters outside President's Office in Al-Etihadiya", (Alnahar Egypt, December 11, 2012) –
Link (in Arabic): https://www.alnaharegypt.com/t~98103

[141] Mohamed Shouman, "Police Officer, Satie Al-Noamany Speakes about Muslim Brotherhood Militia Attacks on Him" (Al-Ahram, Weekly Edition no. 46673, September 19, 2014) –
Link (in Arabic): http://www.ahram.org.eg/NewsQ/326631.aspx

[142] Dalia Ziada, "As turmoil grows in Egypt army rule finds new support" (The National, March 24, 2013) –
Link: https://www.thenational.ae/as-turmoil-grows-in-egypt-army-rule-finds-new-support-1.326251

[143] Mostafa Bakry, "Elsisi: The Road to Retrieving the Egyptian State" (Eldar Almasriah Al-Lebenaniah for publishing, in Arabic, 2014) pp.179-182

[144] ibid, pp. 84-87.

[145] See this video documenting the full statement by Abdel Fattah Elsisi, then the Minister of Defense, and the respective social and political leaders, which announced the end of Muslim Brotherhood's rule in response to street protests:
https://www.youtube.com/watch?v=NHPXvhinCQU

[146] LDI, "Documentary Report I: the Violent Crimes Committed by the Muslim Brotherhood in Egypt between June 30 to December 25, 2013" (Liberal Democracy Institute of Egypt, January 2nd, 2014) –
PDF: https://www.egyldi.org/muslim-brotherhood

[147] Ahmed Abdel Latif, "Kerdasa Massacre of Policemen by Muslim Brotherhood" (Elwatan Newspaper, August 16, 2013) –
Link (in Arabic): https://www.elwatannews.com/news/details/262190

[148] News Report, "Albeltagy: The terrorism in Sinai shall stop as soon as Morsi returns back in power" (Live News Coverage from Rabaa Strike, Al-Nahar TV, July 8, 2013) –
Video (in Arabic): https://www.youtube.com/watch?v=a25hAWTt18Q

[149] Clifford D. May, "Hamas, Muslim Brotherhood manage to fool many people" (Washington Times, May 9, 2017) –
Link: https://www.washingtontimes.com/news/2017/may/9/hamas-muslim-brotherhood-manage-to-fool-many-peopl/

[150] Shaul Shay, "Egypt's War against the Gaza Tunnels" (Israel Defense Journal, February 4, 2018) –
Link: https://www.israeldefense.co.il/en/node/32925

[151] For more information about the conflict and jihadist groups in Sinai, see, for example: Iffat Idris, "Sinai Conflict Analysis" (the UK Department for International Development, The K4D Helpdesk Service, March 2, 2017) –
PDF: http://gsdrc.org/wp-content/uploads/2017/08/049-Sinai-Conflict-Analysis.pdf

[152] For more information on ISIS's Wilayat Sinai structure and dynamics of conflict, see: https://timep.org/esw/non-state-actors/wilayat-sinai/

[153] See reports documenting Muslim Brotherhood's violent atrocities in Egypt, between June 2013 to December 2015, here:
https://www.egyldi.org/muslim-brotherhood

[154] See for example:
- A speech by the Guide of the Muslim Brotherhood, at Rabaa Camp, using verses from Qura'an and Islamic preaching to attack the military institution and claim that Morsi's support is a support to Islam against the enemies of Islam:
https://www.youtube.com/watch?v=mAuHkmXDlxg
- A speech by Safwat Hegazy of the Muslim Brotherhood, at Rabaa Camp, claiming that Prophet Mohamed and Jibril, the angel of God, visited him to bless the participants of Rabaa Strike: https://www.youtube.com/watch?v=GHG5t_gWIcM

[155] See, for example:
- Declassified archives of the Public Prosecutor's investigations, in August 2013, into the militia presence and torture crimes practiced by the Muslim Brotherhood at Rabaa Strike, which led to Public Prosecutor's decision to deploy police forces to evacuate the strike camps: http://www.youm7.com/2842752
- The findings report of the Fact-Finding Mission of the National Council for Human Rights, documenting the incidents of torture and killing of civilians by the Muslim Brotherhood inside the Rabaa camps: https://manshurat.org/node/13664
- The Criminal Court investigations documenting the violent criminal offenses by the Muslim Brotherhood, committed at Rabaa camps, during the sit-in and at the evacuation of the camps on August 14, 2013: http://www.youm7.com/3949974

[156] Ahmed Othman, "The Muslim Brotherhood without Violence Movement Rebels against the Leaders of the Group" (Alarabiya, July 12, 2013) –
Link: https://bit.ly/2S4hApT

[157] Ragab Al-Morshedy, "Muslim Brotherhood Leaders Imprisons and Tortures 670 of the Young Members of Muslim Brotherhood without Violence Movement" (Elwatan Newspaper, July 24, 2013) –
Link: https://www.elwatannews.com/news/details/230965

[158] Hanan Haggag, "The Muslim Brotherhood's exploitation of women" (Al-Ahram Online, English Version, June 29, 2018) - Link: http://english.ahram.org.eg/News/305807.aspx

[159] See, for example, recorded confessions by a young member of the Muslim Brotherhood, revealing how the leaders of the Muslim Brotherhood forced women, at Rabaa Camps, to have sexual relationship with men, in the form of Nikah Jihad. (interview on Sada Elbalad TV, August 13, 2013) –
Video (in Arabic): https://www.youtube.com/watch?v=nYVX2n5MoE8

[160] Ibrahim Ahmed and Hasan Afifi, "Muslim Brotherhood Members Bringing Children from Orphanage Houses in Shubra to Join Rabaa Camps" (Youm7 Newspaper, August 4, 2013) –
Link: http://www.youm7.com/1190833

[161] Mohamed Hegab, "Human Rights Organizations Condemn Muslim Brotherhood's Abuse of Children at Rabaa Strike Camps" (Al-Ahram Daily, August 1, 2013) –
Link: http://www.ahram.org.eg/NewsQ/224150.aspx

[162] See the English translation of Ahmed Almoghier's confessions on the militia training and armament of strikers at Rabaa Camp (Sada Elbalad TV, August, 14, 2016) –
Video: https://www.youtube.com/watch?v=QLA9sP2EwJw

[163] "The full story: Human Rights Delegation's Visit to Rabaa Camp" (Almasry Alyoum, August 2, 2013) –
Link (in Arabic): https://www.almasryalyoum.com/news/details/243933

[164] News Editor, "Egypt Crisis: Morsi's Party Criticizes Al-Azhar's Mediation" (BBC News, Middle East, August 11, 2013) –
Link: https://www.bbc.com/news/world-middle-east-23657288

[165] News Editor, "Egypt crisis: Fears of Failure for Foreign Mediation" (BBC News, Middle East, August 7, 2013) –
Link: https://www.bbc.com/news/world-middle-east-23597860

[166] See, for example, the findings report of the Fact-Finding Mission of the National Council for Human Rights, documenting the incidents of torture and killing of civilians by the Muslim Brotherhood inside the Rabaa camps: https://manshurat.org/node/13664

[167] See this video documenting the first few minutes of the evacuation of Rabaa Strike Camp, showing police forces urging strikers to get out of the strike through a safe exit passage, without being harmed –
Video (in Arabic): https://www.youtube.com/watch?v=YQaysk--fFk

[168] Atef Badr, "A Witness on Rabaa Case to the Criminal Court: The Strikers Killed a Police Officer and We Had to Fight Back" (Almasry Alyoum, June 13, 2017) –
Link: https://www.almasryalyoum.com/news/details/1148041

[169] The Egyptian Ministry of Health announced the official statistics of the victims as follows: Total of 627 people were killed, including civilians and policemen, at several locations all over Egypt, on the day of the evacuation. The number of the people killed at the Rabaa strike camp, including civilians and policemen, were 377 people. Read the Ministry of Health's official press release documenting the statistics, here: https://www.elwatannews.com/news/details/355678

[170] Editor, "UAE Lists Muslim Brotherhood as Terrorist Group" (Reuters, World News, November 15, 2014) –
Link: https://www.reuters.com/article/us-emirates-politics-brotherhood/uae-lists-muslim-brotherhood-as-terrorist-group-idUSKCN0IZ0OM20141115

[171] See for example, The Popular Campaign to Designate the Muslim Brotherhood as a Terrorist Organization:
https://clarionproject.org/delegation-from-egypt-congress-ban-muslim-brotherhood/

[172] Michael Whine, "The Advance of the Muslim Brotherhood in the UK" (Hudson Institute, Government and International Affairs, September 12, 2005) – Link: https://www.hudson.org/research/9845-the-advance-of-the-muslim-brotherhood-in-the-uk

[173] See declassified documents from the FBI investigations on the Muslim Brotherhood's network of charity organizations and financial trusts in the United States, as documented by The Investigative Project on Terrorism, here:
https://www.investigativeproject.org/737/forgotten-investigation-emails-offer-insight-into-iiit-probe

[174] See the Federal Judge decision that CAIR Tied to Hamas, as documented by the Investigative Project on Terrorism, here: https://www.investigativeproject.org/2340/federal-judge-agrees-cair-tied-to-hamas

[175] See for example: Congress' Subcommittee on National Security convened a hearing session, on July 11, 2018, to examine the threat of the Muslim Brotherhood to the United States and its interests and how to effectively counter it.
Video: https://www.youtube.com/watch?v=C8d03tGD2Xg

[176] Declan Walsh, "Trump Talk of Terror Listing for Muslim Brotherhood Alarms Some Arab Allies" (The New York Times, Middle East, February 20, 2017) –
Link: https://www.nytimes.com/2017/02/20/world/middleeast/talk-of-terror-listing-for-muslim-brotherhood-alarms-some-arab-allies.html

[177] Sarah Khan, "Stop fretting over religious sensitivities. We must push hard against Islamists" (The Guardian, June 11, 2017) –
Link: https://www.theguardian.com/commentisfree/2017/jun/10/stop-fretting-over-religious-sensitivities-push-back-against-islamists

[178] GMBWatch, "American Jewish Committee Partners With ISNA" (The Global Muslim Brotherhood Daily Watch, December 5, 2016) –
Link: https://www.globalmbwatch.com/2016/12/05/american-jewish-committee-partners-with-isna/

[179] Mark Hosenball, "Trump administration debates designating Muslim Brotherhood as terrorist group" (Reuters, January 29, 2017) –
Link: https://www.reuters.com/article/us-usa-trump-muslimbrotherhood/trump-administration-debates-designating-muslim-brotherhood-as-terrorist-group-idUSKBN15D0VV

[180] See declassified documents from the FBI investigations on the Muslim Brotherhood's network of charity organizations and financial trusts in the United States, as documented by The Investigative Project on Terrorism, here:
https://www.investigativeproject.org/737/forgotten-investigation-emails-offer-insight-into-iiit-probe

[181] Mohammad Abdel Kader, "Turkey's relationship with the Muslim Brotherhood" (Al-Arabiya Institute for Studies, Perspective, October 14, 2013) –
Link: https://english.alarabiya.net/en/perspective/alarabiya-studies/2013/10/14/Turkey-s-relationship-with-the-Muslim-Brotherhood.html

[182] Editor, "The Islamic veil across Europe" (BBC News, Europe, May 31, 2018) –
Link: https://www.bbc.com/news/world-europe-13038095

[183] The Muslim Brotherhood is listed as an Islamist jihadist organization, by the German Federal Office for the Protection of the Constitution (Bundesamt für Verfassungsschutz) as shown on their website, here: https://www.verfassungsschutz.de/en/fields-of-work/islamism-and-islamist-terrorism/figures-and-facts-islamism/islamist-organisations-2015

[184] Ben Knight, "Al-Jazeera journalist Ahmed Mansour held in Germany on Egyptian warrant" (The Guardian, June 21, 2015) –
Link: https://www.theguardian.com/world/2015/jun/21/ahmed-mansour-germany-detains-al-jazeera-journalist-on-egyptian-warrant

[185] LDI, "Muslim Brotherhood in Britain: Firewall against Violent Extremism or an International Threat?" (Liberal Democracy Institute of Egypt, Documentary Analysis, June 8, 2017) –
Link: https://www.egyldi.org/single-post/2017/06/08/Muslim-Brotherhood-in-Britain-Firewall-against-Violent-Extremism-or-an-International-Threat---Documentary-Analysis

[186] Louisa Loveluck, "Cameron orders investigation into Muslim Brotherhood" (The Telegraph, April 1, 2014) –
Link: https://www.telegraph.co.uk/news/politics/david-cameron/10736490/Cameron-orders-investigation-into-Muslim-Brotherhood.html

[187] Peter Oborne and David Hearst, "UK intelligence had warned against 'fruitless' probe of Muslim Brotherhood" (Middle East Eye, December 17, 2015) - Link: https://www.middleeasteye.net/news/uk-intelligence-had-warned-against-fruitless-probe-muslim-brotherhood-1121433450

[188] Paul Stott, "Analysis: The Islamization of the British Labour Party" (Religious Literacy Institute, November 11, 2016) –
Link: http://religiousliteracyinstitute.org/analysis-islam-labour

[189] Read the full document of the "Muslim Brotherhood Review: Main Findings" published by the House of Commons on December 17, 2015, on this PDF file:
https://web.archive.org/web/20151224103901/https:/www.gov.uk/government/uploads/system/uploads/attachment_data/file/486932/Muslim_Brotherhood_Review_Main_Findings.pdf

[190] Randeep Ramesh, "UAE told UK: crack down on Muslim Brotherhood or lose arms deals" (The Guardian, Middle East, November 6, 2015) –
Link: https://www.theguardian.com/world/2015/nov/06/uae-told-uk-crack-down-on-muslim-brotherhood-or-lose-arms-deals

[191] Vincent Wood, "Muslim Brotherhood members could seek asylum in UK" (Express UK, August 7, 2016) –
Link: https://www.express.co.uk/news/world/697369/Muslim-Brotherhood-uk-asylum-shocking-Home-Office-memo

[192] Read the full report on "Political Islam and the Muslim Brotherhood Review - Sixth Report of Session 2016–17", as published by the House of Commons, Foreign Affairs Committee, on November 1, 2016, on this PDF file:
https://publications.parliament.uk/pa/cm201617/cmselect/cmfaff/118/118.pdf

[193] News Editor, "French appeals court upholds decision to keep Tariq Ramadan in jail" (France 24, August 9, 2018) –
Link: https://www.france24.com/en/20180809-france-tariq-ramadan-loses-appeal-jail

[194] Read the full report on "Political Islam and the Muslim Brotherhood Review - Sixth Report of Session 2016–17", as published by the House of Commons, Foreign Affairs Committee, on November 1, 2016, on this PDF file:
https://publications.parliament.uk/pa/cm201617/cmselect/cmfaff/118/118.pdf

[195] IPT News, "Washington's Schizophrenic Approach Toward the Muslim Brotherhood" (Investigative Project on Terrorism, September 28, 2010) –
Link: https://www.investigativeproject.org/2206/washingtons-schizophrenic-approach-toward

[196] Ayah Aman, "Egypt's youth turn to Islamic State" (Almonitor, November 4, 2014) –
Link: https://www.al-monitor.com/pulse/originals/2014/11/egypt-youth-turn-to-islamic-state-peaceful-brotherhood.html

[197] CEP, "The Muslim Brotherhood's Ties to ISIS and Al-Qaeda" (Counter Extremism Project, Report) –
Link: https://www.counterextremism.com/content/muslim-brotherhood's-ties-isis-and-al-qaeda

[198] Sophia Moskalenko and Clark McCauley, "The Psychology of Lone-wolf terrorism" (Counseling Psychology Quarterly, No.2, 2011)

~~~~~~~~~~~~~~~~~~~~~~~~~~~~~~~~~~~~

Dalia Ziada

The Curious Case of the Three-Legged Wolf

Made in the USA
Middletown, DE
27 November 2023